Enterprise
Cloud Computing

Landmark Books by Meghan-Kiffer Press

DOT.CLOUD:
THE 21ST CENTURY BUSINESS PLATFORM
BUILT ON CLOUD COMPUTING

EXTREME COMPETITION:
INNOVATION AND THE GREAT 21ST CENTURY
BUSINESS REFORMATION

BUSINESS PROCESS MANAGEMENT:
THE THIRD WAVE

POWER IN TE CLOUD:
USING CLOUD COMPUTING
TO BUILD INFORMATION SYSTEMS AT THE EDGE OF CHAOS

IT DOESN'T MATTER:
BUSINESS PROCESSES DO

THE REAL-TIME ENTERPRISE:
COMPETING ON TIME

THE DEATH OF 'E' AND
THE BIRTH OF THE REAL NEW ECONOMY

ENTERPRISE E-COMMERCE

THE BLUEPRINT FOR BUSINESS OBJECTS

NEXT GENERATION COMPUTING:
DISTRIBUTED OBJECTS FOR BUSINESS

Acclaim for Our Books
Featured book recommendation
Harvard Business School's *Working Knowledge,*
Book of the Year, *Internet World*

Meghan-Kiffer Press
Tampa, Florida, USA
www.mkpress.com
Innovation at the Intersection of Business and Technology

Some Early Thoughts on Cloud Computing

"The world has been reset. Today's uncertainty feels like the 'new normal.' We will not return to the relative tranquility of the pre-crisis world. Growth will be harder to come by, trends will be more volatile and constituent voices will be louder. We see this environment as an opportunity to renew GE." [1]
—Jeffrey Immelt, CEO, General Electric, March, 2010.

"The Cloud will do for government what the Internet did in the 1990s. We're interested in consumer technology for the enterprise. It's a fundamental change to the way our government operates."
—Vivek Kundra, CIO, the U.S. Government [2]

"The rise of the Cloud is more than just another platform shift that gets geeks excited. It will undoubtedly transform the IT industry, but it will also profoundly change the way people work and companies operate." —*The Economist*, "Let it Rise."

"We really don't want to operate datacenters anymore. We'd rather spend our time giving our customers great service and writing great software than managing physical hardware."
—Don MacAskill, CEO, SmugMug

"Undoubtedly, cloud computing will continue to grow in the years ahead. And when industry observers of the future look back at these early days of adoption, they'll recognize the tectonic shift caused by cloud computing, which has both transformed enterprise IT delivery and established the Internet as an effective enterprise computing platform."
—Ric Telford, Vice President, Cloud Services, IBM.[3]

"The Cloud makes it possible to deliver everything as a service—from business processes to personal interactions; and to create altogether new business models across industries. In my view, the

ability to facilitate innovation and entrepreneurship in this new model is one of the most promising ways to ignite the next wave of economic growth. We can no more see the full impact of the Cloud than Henry Ford foresaw the impact of his desire to produce more cars in less time."
—Russ Daniels, VP and CTO of Cloud Services Strategy at HP.

"A ship in a harbor is safe, but that is not what a ship is built for."
—Computing Pioneer, Grace Hooper.

"Everything is up for grabs. Everything will change. There is a magnificent sweep of intellectual landscape right in front of us. The network is the computer—yes; but we're less interested in computers all the time. The real topic in astronomy is the cosmos, not telescopes. The real topic in computing is the Cybersphere, not the computers we use as telescopes and tuners."
—Yale Professor David Gelernter, *The Second Coming*, 2000.

"The Cloud is a framework for the disruption of structure, a place where we will all live, work and play. Describing the full impact that the Cloud will have would be paramount to explaining the effects of jet lag to a 17th century, horse-bound traveler."
—Thomas Koulopoulos, CEO, Delphi Group.

"I love the fact that I don't need to deal with servers, staging, version maintenance, security, and performance."
—Jon Williams, CIO of Kaplan Test Prep and Admission. [4]

"It's got to be secure as we do this. This is our lives. The computing industry's move to sell pay-as-you-go computing cycles available as a service on the Internet is 'a security nightmare,' and it cannot be handled in traditional ways."
—John Chambers, CEO, Cisco [5]

"There are always important business issues forming like storm clouds on the horizon, but that are not yet so potent that they seem to demand your concerted attention. However, this is precisely the best time to focus on these issues and decide whether you should put more resources against them—right now. By doing so, you can gain an advantage over your competitors who haven't even glanced at the horizon yet or, if they have, are waiting to see what develops before they take any action. The danger is that, if you don't look ahead, those emerging wisps of vapor can rapidly turn into fast-moving thunderheads that hit before you've lifted a finger, especially if a competitor has taken action.

—George Stalk, Boston Consulting Group, *Five Future Strategies You Need Right Now.*

References.

[1] http://www.reuters.com/article/idUSTRE6243OD20100305

[2] http://www.nextgov.com/nextgov/ng_20081126_1117.php

[3] http://news.zdnet.com/2100-9595_22-330238.html

[4] http://news.zdnet.com/2100 9595_22-330238.html

[5]

http://www.csoonline.com/article/490368/Cisco_CEO_Cloud_Computing_a_Security_Nightmare_

Enterprise Cloud Computing

A Strategy Guide for Business and Technology Leaders —and the Rest of Us

Andy Mulholland
Jon Pyke
Peter Fingar

Meghan-Kiffer Press
Tampa, Florida, USA, www.mkpress.com
Innovation at the Intersection of Business and Technology

Publisher's Cataloging-in-Publication Data

Mulholland, Andy.
Enterprise Cloud Computing: A Strategy Guide of Business and Technology Leaders
/ Andy Mulholland, Jon Pyke, Peter Fingar, - 1st ed.
p. cm.
  Includes bibliographic entries, appendices, and index.
  ISBN-10: 0-929652-29-0   ISBN-13: 978-0-929652-29-0

  1. Management 2. Technological innovation. 3. Diffusion of innovations.
  4. Globalization—Economic aspects. 5. Information technology. 6. Information Society. 7. Organizational change. I. Mulholland, Andy. II. Title

HM48.M75 2010   Library of Congress No. 2010927050
303.48'33–dc22   CIP

Published by Meghan-Kiffer Press
310 East Fern Street — Suite G
Tampa, FL 33604 USA

Any product mentioned in this book may be a trademark of its
company.

Meghan-Kiffer books are available at special quantity discounts for
corporate education and training use. For more information, write
Special Sales, Meghan-Kiffer Press, Suite G, 310 East Fern Street,
Tampa, Florida 33604, or email info@mkpress.com

MK

Meghan-Kiffer Press
Tampa, Florida, USA
Innovation at the Intersection of Business and Technology

Printed in the United States of America.
MK Printing 10 9 8 7 6 5 4 3 2 1   SAN 249-7980

Table of Contents

PREFACE 11

1. PROLOG AND A BRIEF FAQ 15
    AUDIENCE FOR THIS BOOK 17
    AN ENTERPRISE CLOUD COMPUTING FAQ 17

2. THERE'S "NO SUCH THING" AS CLOUD COMPUTING 23
    KEY POINTS: SOME WORKING DEFINITIONS 23
    DEFINITION OF CLOUD COMPUTING 26
    WHY IS CLOUD COMPUTING SO HARD TO UNDERSTAND? 40
    ENTERPRISE USE CASE SCENARIOS 44
    ADDITIONAL BACKGROUND CONCEPTS 45
    THE LARGER ECONOMIC CONTEXT: THE PERFECT STORM 52
    TAKEAWAY 54

3. WELCOME TO THE HUMAN NETWORK 57
    KEY POINTS: THE CONNECTED SOCIETY IS CHANGING HOW BUSINESSES
    OPERATE 57
    BEING IN THE KNOW 60
    IT'S A MATTER OF TRUST 63
    DID YOU KNOW? 64
    SOCIAL CONSTRUCTIONISM AND COLLECTIVISM 65
    SOCIAL NETWORKS AS A PLACE WHERE WORK GETS DONE 69
    SOCIAL NETWORKS AS A PLACE WHERE INNOVATION GETS DONE 71
    TO TWITTER OR NOT TO TWITTER 74
    HOW BIG AND HOW POWERFUL IS THE SOCIAL WEB? 78
    PUTTING IT ALL TOGETHER 80
    TAKEAWAY 82

4. FROM INFORMATION TECHNOLOGY TO
    BUSINESS TECHNOLOGY 85
    KEY POINTS: FROM TRANSACTIONS TO INTERACTIONS 85
    A MESH OF CONNECTIONS 86
    THE RELATIONSHIPS AMONG EXISTING AND NEW TECHNOLOGIES 88
    IT'S NOT ABOUT CLOUD *COMPUTING*, IT'S ABOUT CLOUD *SERVICES* .. 93
    GOING MOBILE 96
    LOOK MA, NO COMPUTER 101
    SOCIAL COMPANIES 102
    REARRANGING THE FURNITURE FOR THE CLOUD ERA 104

TAKEAWAY 106

5. THE SERVICE-ORIENTED ENTERPRISE IN THE CLOUD .109

KEY POINTS: WHAT DOES A CLOUD-POWERED ENTERPRISE LOOK LIKE?
.... 109
BUSINESS FACES PRESSING ISSUES 110
WHY IS SOE COMPELLING? 112
WHAT IS A SOE AND WHAT DOES IT LOOK LIKE? 114
THE RE-BIRTH OF SERVICE-ORIENTED ARCHITECTURE (SOA) 117
WHAT THE TRANSFORMATION OPPORTUNITY LOOKS LIKE 125
THE DYNAMICS OF THE BUSINESS TRANSFORMATION 126
TAKEAWAY: HOW TO DELIVER THE SOE COLLABORATIVELY 127

6. BUSINESS PROCESS MANAGEMENT IN THE CLOUD 131

KEY POINTS: THE PROCESS-DRIVEN ENTERPRISE 131
CHANGE AND THE ORGANIZATION 131
THE EMERGENCE OF BUSINESS PROCESS MANAGEMENT SYSTEMS ... 133
NEXT GENERATION BPM: THE BUSINESS OPERATIONS PLATFORM ... 136
SITUATIONAL APPLICATIONS: THE OPPORTUNITY OR THE THREAT FOR
BUSINESS TECHNOLOGY 141
SITUATIONAL BUSINESS PROCESSES AND CHOREOGRAPHY 143
PROCESS ON DEMAND – FANTASY OR FAST TRACK TO AGILITY? 151
SERVICES AS A SERVICE 156
TAKEAWAY 162

7. ENTERPRISE CLOUD COMPUTING: THE PROCESS 165

KEY POINTS: THE SUCCESSFUL ADOPTION PROCESS 165
FUNDING MODELS AT THE HEART OF WEATHERING CURRENT
ECONOMIC CONDITIONS 166
YOUR ENTERPRISE IS WHAT IT COMMUNICATES 168
DON'T CLIMB DANGEROUS MOUNTAINS WITHOUT A GUIDE 170
CHARACTERISTICS OF SUCCESSFUL TECHNOLOGY ADOPTION 172
LEGACY SYSTEMS CONTINUE TO ADD VALUE 172
DEVELOPERS APPLY NEW SKILLS TO NEW CHALLENGES 176
ARCHITECTURAL THINKING ALLOWS FOR CHANGE 179
A SUCCESSFUL TECHNOLOGY ADOPTION PROCESS 185
TAKEAWAY 199

8. EPILOG 201

APPENDICES

A. CLOUD COMPUTING USE CASES **205**

END USER TO CLOUD 205
ENTERPRISE TO CLOUD TO END USER 205
ENTERPRISE TO CLOUD.. 207
ENTERPRISE TO CLOUD TO ENTERPRISE 208
PRIVATE CLOUD 209
CHANGING CLOUD VENDORS 210
HYBRID CLOUD 212
CONCLUSIONS AND RECOMMENDATIONS 214

**B. HOW TO EVOLVE
YOUR IRRELEVANT CORPORATE WEB SITE** **217**

C. GLOBAL COLLECTIVIST SOCIETY IS COMING ONLINE 221

D. ROI FOR SOCIAL NETWORKS **227**

E. WEB RESOURCES.. **229**

F. JERICHO FORUM COMMANDMENTS **233**

G. BRIEF GLOSSARY OF NIST DEFINITIONS........................... **239**

BIBLIOGRAPHY **243**

SOCIAL MEDIA 243
WEB 2.0.. 246
CLOUD COMPUTING... 248
SERVICE-ORIENTED ARCHITECTURE (SOA)...................... 250
BUSINESS PROCESS MANAGEMENT 253

INDEX.. **256**

ABOUT THE AUTHORS.. **263**

Preface

We didn't sit down and decide to write this book.
It was born of necessity.

While there are many unanswered questions about the new IT buzzword "cloud computing," modern businesses are under assault. Driven by the globalization of markets, extreme competition and unexpected change, companies are now seeking radical changes in the ways they organize work and conduct business. The new way of competing demands a sharper focus on customers, cost-cutting, quality and constant adaptability.

At stake is nothing less than survival.

While cloud computing is recognized as an essential enabler of business reinvention, it's not yet clear how to find your way through all of the industry's hype and fog to apprehend its true potential. After all, it turns out that there is no such "thing" as cloud computing:

- It's not a new technology.
- It's not a new architecture.
- It's not a new methodology.

It is, however, a new means of delivering IT resources, and that very simple statement speaks volumes.

With the complete fusion of technology into the modern enterprise, technology and business have become inseparable. Together they are needed to address the bigger world, the bigger society, in which a business must operate. And it's that bigger world that has changed as a result of the hyper-connectivity of the Internet that, in turn, has given rise to Social Networks where the future is being discussed, debated and transformed.

As unlikely book producers, the three of us have been at the front lines of business technology for several decades, bringing 120 years of combined experience to the table. As *doers*, not academics, we don't just talk about what's happening with cloud computing and its transformational power, we are deeply involved in working in this new environment.

It's our experience gained from *doing* that gave birth to this book. However, we don't claim to have all the answers. But we do ask the right questions. Our clients and colleagues challenged us to share the lessons learned from out frontline experience. This is precisely what we humbly seek to accomplish in these pages.

It may surprise you that we devote a great deal of attention to changes going on in the larger world, the larger society, outside the traditional supply-and-demand business world.

We believe that it's the social constructivism emerging in our wired world that has huge consequences for business, even to the point of what it means to be a business.

So if you are looking for a bunch of techno-speak, look elsewhere. While we do not avoid technological terminology, we do our best to explain relevant technology concepts in everyday language, for our intended audience is composed of business leaders and everyone else that in some way have responsibility for charting the future of their organizations. So along the way we'll describe, in lay terms, some of the enabling technologies that are required to move from concept to reality.

But this book is not about those technologies. It's not for programmers or technologists looking for technical guidance or programming recipes.

It's about how cloud computing is being forged with new categories of resources and services that give business people control over their business processes to compete for the future—a future that's certainly not business as usual.

In short, we strive to close the knowledge gap faced by our clients and colleagues. We aspire to inform, to educate and to foster understanding of the next generation of computing in business, the cloud computing generation. Guiding principles for this book include:

- Make a strong business case, not just a strong technology case.
- Do not trivialize, hype or oversell the concepts.
- Make the content relevant to business people.
- Take the readers from where they are to today to where they

can be with cloud computing.

As a learning instrument, this book belongs to *you*, the reader. This is primarily a book for business people, for at its core it's about how cloud computing can and must be mastered by the enterprise that wants to win in the decade ahead.

Please read, enjoy and learn.

And please take advantage of the many resources provided in the appendices to continue your journey.

Andy Mulholland
Jon Pyke
Peter Fingar

May 2010

1. Prolog and a Brief FAQ

If you have an email account with Yahoo, Google or Hotmail, or if you have a blog or an account with Facebook, congratulations, you are a pioneer and early adopter of cloud computing!

Cloud computing is all the rage these days and one of the most hyped terms to come along in the past decade. What is it? That depends on who you ask. It seems almost any form of information technology has been rebranded as cloud computing if it has anything to do with the Internet. The term is interpreted as broadly as the term "computing" itself. The literature on the topic is exploding, and cloud computing has stirred the imagination of pundits, commentators and analysts—it's:

- A 21st century megatrend
- A framework for the disruption of structure
- The great economic leveler
- A global social and economic network
- The disruption of industrial nations
- The democratization of the media
- The beginning of the end of nation states
- The rise of a truly global village
- The enabler of global terrorism
- The enabler of the power shift from West to East
- The next evolution in the history of computing
- The convergence of digital and physical worlds

Well, as we are neither pundits nor analysts, we'll leave the job of predictions to them. Maybe in ten years or so we can look back and evaluate what happened today in a more objective way. Just not today. While there's no doubt that cloud computing will have a major impact on the world, it's far too early to make grand predictions. But it's already past time for enterprises large and small to understand basic constructs and come to grips with cloud computing. Although the underlying technologies and standards will rapidly evolve, the impact of cloud computing on the enterprise is here and now.

The opening paragraph above is a reference to *consumer-level* cloud computing, call it Consumer IT if you like. But what's gone missing in much of the literature so far is a discussion of what cloud computing means for the enterprise and what business leaders should be thinking and doing to address this 21st century megatrend. That's precisely the intent of this book. It's an *enterprise-level* treatment of cloud computing, along with some practical guidance—all in non-technical language and free of jargon as much as possible. Where technical terms are used, they are explained in everyday language.

> To repeat what we wrote in the Preface,
> this is not a technical book about cloud computing,
> nor is it an implementation guide full of checklists.
> Existing architectural, development and governance methods are
> well established in large enterprises, and those need not be
> replaced. Rather they will need to be adjusted or refactored to
> accommodate the special elements of cloud computing such as
> taking an outside-in versus inside-out approach to issues such as
> security, governance and policy management.

This book provides an examination of the megatrends in the larger world outside of the business world that have come about as a result of the world being hyper-connected in real time by the Internet. In this context we explore the needed shifts that businesses must consider to prepare for 21st century competition. In this book we:

- Examine what cloud computing is in order to set the context for what it means for the enterprise.
- Look at the newly emerged participatory society and how it's changing the ways businesses must operate in order to survive.
- Describe the needed shift from Information Technology (IT) to Business Technology (BT).
- Provide the rationale for a Service-Oriented Enterprise that operates in the Cloud.
- Explain the business process management (BPM) requirements

of enterprise cloud computing that sets it apart from consumer-level cloud computing.

- Set forth a high-level process for the adoption of cloud computing in the enterprise. We specifically avoid cookie-cutter checklist approaches as each organization is unique in its requirements, culture and technological capabilities. Throwing out existing business and IT disciplines because of cloud computing isn't just a bad idea, it's a really bad idea. Why? Because cloud computing is *not* a new technology, architecture or methodology, medium and large enterprises will use and extend, not replace, their architectural processes and development methods.

Audience for This Book

We reiterate, this book is about what the Cloud portends for business, and what companies should be thinking and doing about the biggest shift since the advent of the Internet itself.

Anyone interested in cloud computing should read this book if they are in any way involved with business or government organizations (consultants, employees, enterprise architects, technologists and strategists). *Enterprise Cloud Computing* is designed to provide insights and guidance for people who are in some way responsible for the future of their organizations including CEOs, CIOs, CFOs, CMOs and other C-level executives. It will also be useful to IT staff in order to gain common ground with non-technical people on the business issues related to cloud computing.

An Enterprise Cloud Computing FAQ

As a quick warm-up and indication of the learning objectives for this book, here is a short list of frequently asked questions (FAQ) related to enterprise cloud computing:

What is "cloud computing?"

The U.S. National Institute of Standards and Technology provides the most neutral definition of cloud computing. "Cloud computing is a model for enabling convenient, on-demand network access to a shared pool of configurable computing resources (e.g., networks, servers, storage, applications and services) that can be rapidly provisioned and released with minimal management effort or service provider interaction. This cloud model promotes availability and is composed of five essential characteristics, three delivery models, and four deployment models."

What is enterprise *cloud computing?*

Enterprise cloud computing is the special case of utilizing cloud computing for competitive advantage through breakout opportunities both for cost savings and, more importantly, for business innovation in terms of unprecedented speed and agility with vastly improved collaboration among business partners and customers.

What does "cloud computing" mean for the enterprise?

More important than the question of "what is it?" is why it matters. Here are three key points. 1) On the cost side of the equation, many, but not all, IT and data center costs can be reduced and tied directly to usage, up or down as needs go up or down (rapid elasticity). 2) But there's more, much more, on the revenue side. Risk and startup expenses for innovation initiatives can be cut dramatically, letting companies take more small bets and test out more new ideas. With no upfront capital expense, new projects can be scaled up instantly if they take off, or shut down quickly if they fail. Massive scalability and up-or-down elasticity give companies a whole new sandbox for testing new business ideas and growing them if they take off. 3) Companies don't work alone, and, on average, over 20 companies make up today's value chains. Cloud computing allows a company to collaborate in new ways with its trading partners, and collaboration is the key to gaining competitive advantage across the value chain. By establishing shared workspaces in "Community Clouds" employees from multiple companies can work together as a "virtual enterprise network" and function as though they were a single company. They all participate in the same value delivery system, sharing computing, communication and information resources. This is especially important as no one company "owns" the overall value chain.

Is cloud computing new?

Cloud computing is *not* a new technology or architecture or methodology. But it *is* a new Information Technology "delivery model" where all computing and networking resources are delivered as "services" that are elastic (use as much or as little as you need at any given time), massively scalable, and are available on-demand with self-service, pay-as-you-go variable cost subscriptions.

What's driving enterprise cloud computing?

For sure, cost savings represent a significant driver. But far more important are the changes going on in the larger world outside of the business world in our hyper-connected global society. With the advent of easy-to-use "Consumer IT" or Web 2.0 usage of the Internet, Social Networks are changing the ways we live, learn, collaborate, work, consume and play. These huge changes in society also disrupt the way we design and manage our organizations and our value chains that deliver value to customers.

What is a Service-Oriented Enterprise?

What really differentiates a Service-Oriented Enterprise (SOE) from a traditional business model is its "outside-in" approach. A SOE creates business-driven value by defining and exposing its core business processes to the external market through the use of open technology in the form of "services." This reorganization includes new business requirements, new operating zones and new license structures that can enable improved collaboration between organizations and their customers and suppliers. A SOE has the capability to organize its responses to market shifts due to the agility within its culture, processes and IT systems.

What is Business Technology?

The term Business Technology (BT) is frequently used to describe new technologies such as Web 2.0 and their use in business to differentiate them from the tools and techniques of traditional Information Technology (IT). The key differentiation between BT and IT centers on decentralization and unstructured environments. Organizations still need the centralized and structured role of IT to

provide back office functionality, but BT is an additional layer focusing on the front office and customer-facing business activities.

Is cloud computing the same as Software-as-a-Service(SaaS)?

While SaaS vendors originally did not use the word "cloud" to describe their offerings, analysts now consider SaaS to be one of several subsets of the cloud computing market. With traditional SaaS
offerings, a company is buying pre-packaged "canned" software
applications (e.g., ERP, SCM or CRM packages) that are hosted
remotely, usually in a multitenancy environment, and accessed via
the Internet. SaaS applications can become "participants" in unique
end-to-end business processes (see BPMaaS).

What is Business Process Management as a Service (BPMaaS)?

With SaaS offerings, a company is buying "same-old" pre-packaged
software, but BPMaaS goes far beyond canned "business software
as usual" being put online. It goes on to creating unique business
processes designed for unique and specific purposes to link together multi-company value delivery systems that in the past weren't
feasible or economical to join together. BPMaaS is all about the
complete management of business processes, and puts business
people in charge of their processes. In many ways, BPMaaS is what
sets *enterprise cloud computing* apart from *consumer cloud computing*.
Unique business processes are how companies differentiate themselves, and are thus paramount to the enterprise use of cloud computing for competitive advantage. BPMaaS covers the full lifecycle
of business processes, from their conception, design implementation and optimization. Bringing BPM capabilities to the Cloud
enables multiple companies to share a common BPM system and
fully participate in an overall end-to-end business process.

What are the economics of cloud computing?

Cloud computing brings immense economies of scale to computing and delivers computing resources on-demand in much the
same way utilities deliver gas and electricity. In the past, companies
had to make ever-growing capital expenditures (CAPEX) in com-

puting resources to implement new information systems. Furthermore, to accommodate potential peak loads, they installed huge amounts of capacity so that today only 10-15% of data center capacity is typical utilized. The shift to the on-demand model of cloud computing isn't just about cost savings. Far more important, it's about giving organizations the agility they need to act quickly on new opportunities without IT being on the critical path. "Fast to market" is a central economic variable and speed is essential in the world of total global competition.

What's the difference between "cloud computing" and "cloud services?"

In short, everything. "Cloud computing" implies a framework and vocabulary aimed at technology semantics. "Cloud services" implies a framework and vocabulary aimed at business semantics. While cloud computing belongs to the domain of Information Technology (IT), cloud services belong to the domain of Business Technology (BT). In other words, cloud services are about business, while cloud computing is about technology. The focus of this book is on the domain of business.

2. There's "No Such Thing" As Cloud Computing

Key Points: Some Working Definitions

To be sure, cost savings are an important part of any cloud computing discussion and the topic is covered throughout the literature. On the other hand, the Cloud isn't just about data center consolidations and pay-per-drink cost savings; it's about transforming an enterprise. This chapter provides key concepts and a baseline vocabulary to establish the context for our later discussions.

Note: We initially set this chapter to be an appendix, for our goal isn't to define and elaborate on what cloud computing "is" but rather to focus on what it means to the enterprise and what organizations should be thinking and doing. In our initial approach we deferred to the National Institute of Standards and Technology (NIST) for a basic definition, assuming most readers will already have an understanding of what cloud computing is. However, after much feedback and discussion, we decided to set baseline definitions for our overall discussion to establish context and to extend the basic NIST model with important components relevant to Enterprise Cloud Computing versus a more general notion of the subject. For example we expand on the NIST model to include business process management and management controls "as a Service" (BPMaaS and MCaaS). So if you already have a good understanding of what cloud computing is, just skim this chapter and pause to review our discussion of BPMaaS and MCaaS.

The IT industry has a history of self-proclaiming a "disruption" with the advent of new technologies and solutions, but only a select few have withstood the test of time and proven to be genuinely disruptive. Now comes "cloud computing."
But wait, cloud computing isn't a "thing:"
- It's not a new technology.
- It's not a new IT architecture.
- It's not a new methodology.

"What the hell is Cloud Computing? I have no idea what anybody is talking about. I mean it is really just complete gibberish. It's insane."—Larry Ellison, CEO, Oracle Corporation, September 2008.

> The big deal is that cloud computing
> is a disruptive *delivery* model.
> It's an economic, not technological shift!

Established Cloud Service Providers (CSPs) already offer a wide range of operating systems, database management systems, and application servers. Even email and desktop productivity packages are available in the Cloud, offering significant cost advantages over supplying these services in-house.

General Electric switched over 400,000 desktops and the city of Washington, D.C. has moved its 38,000 desktops to an internal Cloud. (See the Forrester report, "Should Your Email Live In The Cloud? A Comparative Cost Analysis," in the footnote reference).[1]

But there's much more than moving desktops to the Cloud, including immediate mission-critical requirements, not for some garage startup, but for the U.S. Department of Defense. One of many visions for government cloud computing was played out for real in the aftermath of Haiti's 2010 earthquake. In the absence of basic communications networks, the Defense Information Systems Agency's Rapid Access Computing Environment (RACE) became the network platform for relief workers to share information in the impoverished nation of Haiti. The agency was able to put a network infrastructure into place at *the speed of heat* using the cloud-based system. RACE normally provides on-demand computing capabilities for the military, but in Haiti, military and nongovernmental groups used it to provide a network. It provided a diverse group of users situational awareness that allowed people to chat and build courses of action.

The RACE Cloud service platform and readily-available software applications permitted relief workers to establish collaboration services, providing an example of how recent technology and social media innovations can revolutionize the way government works with citizens. The DISA Cloud service enabled relief workers to locate Creole translators and counselors throughout the world to help respond to text requests for help.

The success of RACE is just one part of DISA's broader efforts to move away from a platform-centric approach in providing computing and communications services, to one that is focused on providing enterprise-level services across its entire network, whenever and wherever its military customers need them. This network-centric enterprise service does not mean just being on the network. Instead, it means being standards-based, platform neutral, interoperable and interdependent. The goal is to store information in the Cloud and make it discoverable and accessible to whomever needs it virtually anywhere in the world.

Behind those services is an emphasis on service-oriented architecture that takes into account the need for universal connectivity, whether it's person-to-person, person-to-machine, or machine-to-machine. It also takes into account the importance of taxonomies and labeling to make information easy to discover and capable of being delivered in the right format, anywhere, at any time.

Meanwhile, incumbent providers of enterprise systems such as enterprise resource planning (ERP) are quickly becoming CSPs: Oracle, SAP and Netsuite, to name a few. Over the last decade or so ERP systems have become mainstays of large corporations, even with their baggage of expensive installation, configuration and maintenance costs.

These examples are but the tip of the iceberg as organizations of all sizes learn how cloud computing can go far beyond desktop applications and pre-packaged enterprise software and impact every aspect of IT. For example, Lockheed Martin has deployed a Cloud-based Collaborative Engineering system to orchestrate the work of hundreds of subcontractors that have disparate product lifecycle management (PLM) and CAD/CAM systems. This represents one of the world's most complex enterprise computing environments now being addressed by cloud computing. This later point brings us to the major theme of this book ...

The wow about cloud computing isn't about on-demand IT.
It's about on-demand Business Innovation.

Definition of Cloud Computing

With so much hype surrounding cloud computing, and with 40 definitions coming from 40 different experts who are asked what cloud computing is, we'll not add to the fray in this book. But, as this book addresses no-nonsense business executives responsible for the success of their organizations, we need a baseline definition devoid of bias. So, we turn to the Information Technology Laboratory of the National Institute of Standards and Technology (NIST), an agency of the United States Department of Commerce. The NIST Cloud Computing Project led by Peter Mell has posted its working definition of cloud computing. Computer scientists at NIST developed the draft definition in collaboration with industry and government organizations. It was developed as the foundation for a special publication on Cloud architectures, security and deployment strategies for the federal government.

Cloud computing is a model for enabling convenient, on-demand network access to a shared pool of configurable computing resources (e.g., networks, servers, storage, applications, and services) that can be rapidly provisioned and released with minimal management effort or service provider interaction. This cloud model promotes availability and is composed of five essential *characteristics*, three *delivery models*, and four *deployment models*.

Note 1: Cloud computing is still an evolving paradigm. Its definitions, use cases, underlying technologies, issues, risks, and benefits will be refined in a spirited debate by the public and private sectors. These definitions, attributes, and characteristics will evolve and change over time.

Note 2: The cloud computing industry represents a large ecosystem of many models, vendors, and market niches. This definition attempts to encompass all of the various cloud approaches.

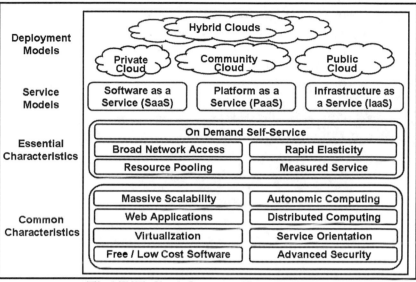

The NIST Cloud Computing Framework [2]

Essential Characteristics

- *On-demand self-service.* A consumer can provision computing capabilities, such as server time and network storage, as needed automatically without requiring human interaction with each service's provider [self-provisioning of resources].
- *Ubiquitous network access.* Capabilities are available over the network and accessed through standard mechanisms that promote use by heterogeneous thin or thick client platforms (e.g., mobile phones, laptops, and PDAs).
- *Location independent resource pooling.* The provider's computing resources are pooled to serve all consumers using a multi-tenant model, with different physical and virtual resources dynamically assigned and reassigned according to consumer demand. The customer generally has no control or knowledge over the exact location of the provided resources but may be able to specify location at a specific country, state, or data center. Examples include storage, processing, memory, network bandwidth, and virtual machines.
- *Rapid elasticity.* Capabilities can be rapidly and elastically provisioned to quickly scale up and rapidly released to quickly scale

down. To the consumer, the capabilities available for provisioning often appear to be infinite [massive scalability, supercomputer power on demand] and can be purchased in any quantity at any time.

- *Measured Service.* Cloud systems automatically control and optimize resource use by leveraging a metering capability appropriate to the type of service (e.g., storage, processing, bandwidth, and active user accounts). Resource usage can be monitored, controlled and reported providing transparency for both the provider and consumer of the service (a pay-as-you-go model).

Note: Cloud software takes full advantage of the Cloud paradigm by being service oriented with a focus on statelessness, low coupling, modularity, and semantic interoperability.

Delivery Models

The central concept and language used for cloud computing essentially relates to supplying "Everything as a Service."

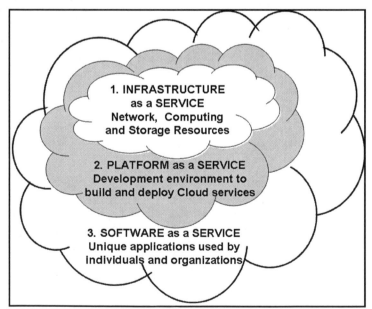

Everything as a Service

- *1. Cloud Infrastructure as a Service (IaaS).* The capability provided to the consumer is to provision processing, storage, networks, and other fundamental computing resources where the consumer is able to deploy and run arbitrary software which can include operating systems and applications. The consumer does not manage or control the underlying cloud infrastructure but has control over operating systems, storage, deployed applications, and possibly select networking components (e.g., firewalls, load balancers).

To amplify on the NIST definition, IaaS is the base-level provisioning of pure technology elements, most commonly meaning a hosting service provider such as Google or Amazon that provides so-called "virtual machines" on demand with payment geared to the amount of usage. This means that the time and cost of procuring and installing actual physical machines at the client's premises is avoided and what behaves as a single machine is made available across the Internet. The term "virtual machine" means that a portion of a server farm or compute grid is made available as a separate machine from the user's perspective. In the IaaS model each increase in required capacity is matched by an increase in the resources made available, and the resources are wound down when they are no longer required (rapid elasticity). Services are billed only for the resources consumed, and may include combinations of CPU hours, millions of instructions per second (Mips), bandwidth, and storage.

Companies are always looking for ways to run existing applications that decrease the cost of providing technology infrastructures—and this usually means running on IaaS. There is a great deal of debate about what applications can be moved safely outside the Firewall to remote hosting services. Increasingly, small and medium enterprises are driving toward this change, but larger enterprises with existing in-house IT teams are more reluctant and would choose the more costly route of traditional data center and operational outsourcing rather than risk shared hosted environments. In many cases they will deploy private internal Clouds or implement a Virtual Private Cloud (VPC) hosted by a Cloud services provider.

- *2. Cloud Platform as a Service (PaaS).* This capability provides the consumer the means to develop applications using programming languages and tools supported by the Cloud services provider (e.g., Java, Python, .Net). The consumer does not manage or control the underlying cloud infrastructure, network, servers, operating systems, or storage, but the consumer has control over the deployed applications and possibly application hosting environment configurations.

To expand on the NIST definition, PaaS introduces the next level of sophistication by moving beyond simple technology elements that need to be configured into operational systems or platforms. It provides the capability to have "services" (as opposed to applications) loaded directly on to the platform. Such platforms can be pre-configured to support a specific programming language in a "standard" hosting environment. Platforms can be built for specific use by an industry or an enterprise, complete with management and governance capabilities. However, the most common type of PaaS is the type that provides a core set of services to which a wide range of additional services can be added to leverage the core services. An example of this is the Force.com platform offering Salesforce.com customer relationship management (CRM) as a core set of services to which developers can add services for special purposes that extend the original core set of services. Another example is the Cordys Business Operations Platform (BOP) where the capabilities of a full lifecycle business process management system can be extended with "processes on demand."

- *3. Cloud Software as a Service (SaaS)* The capability provided to the consumer is to use the provider's applications running on a cloud infrastructure and accessible from various client devices through a thin client interface such as a Web browser. The consumer does not manage or control the underlying cloud infrastructure, network, servers, operating systems, storage, or individual application capabilities, with the possible exception of limited user-specific application configuration settings.

To amplify on the NIST definition, SaaS can be implemented in the Cloud model (and thereby realizing the economic benefits), or by hosting separate instances that are not based on the Cloud paradigm. For example, a large SaaS provider can host separate instances of, let's say its CRM system, one for each customer. This is more expensive than the implementation where a single instance hosts all customers (multitenacy). The costs of the former would be one or two orders of magnitude more expensive per seat, even with virtualization, due to the increased complexity, licensing costs and so on. The multitenant model also offers advantages such as when upgrades to security or other software features occur, they apply to all clients.

SaaS is the delivery of actual end-user functionality, either as "services" grouped together and orchestrated to perform the required functionality or as a conventional monolithic application. It is in this layer that the really important differentiations are found.

The real driver for SaaS is not traditional IT applications; it's the "edge of the enterprise" where business users require a flexible model to deploy new technologies to improve front office performance. The key significance is that while IT has a major role in the enterprise back office (transaction processing and systems of record), these new requirements are directly associated with "go-to-market" activities and will be subject to constant change. These new requirements must be met very quickly for competitive purposes; they are likely to endure for only a few months; and their costs will be directly attributed to the business units consuming the needed "services." The flexibility of "services" that can be rapidly changed, the availability of PaaS on which to base the services, and the costing model, all contribute to the creation of the SaaS market, which in turn, drives the PaaS and IaaS markets.

But wait!

There's more to the three Software-Platform-Infrastructure (SPI) layers that NIST addresses when it comes to *enterprise cloud computing.*

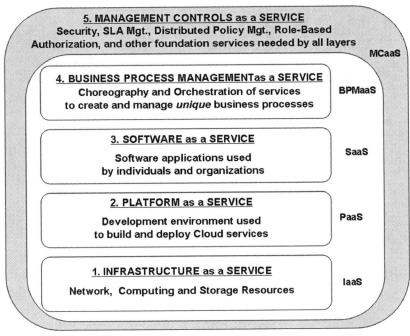

Expanded Delivery Model

- 4. *Business Process Management as a Service (BPMaaS).* Sometimes referred to as Process as a Service (PraaS) or Business Process as a Service (BPaaS), BPM services represent the highest functional level in the Cloud services hierarchy. These services provide the complete end-to-end business process management capabilities needed for the creation and follow-on management of unique business processes.

What's the difference between SaaS and BPMaaS? There's much more with BPMaaS. With SaaS offerings, a company is buying the "same-ole" packaged software (though initially configurable), and the "much more" goes far beyond canned "business software as usual" being put online. It goes on to creating unique business processes designed for unique purposes to link together multi-company value delivery systems that in the past weren't feasible or economical to join together. Call them "situational business processes" if you like, and we'll elaborate on this idea in later chapters. Fortunately, those "canned SaaS applications" can become "participants" (or components) in end-to-end business processes that can deliver business innovation on demand.

> BPMaaS is all about the *complete management of business processes* and makes it possible to place the control of business processes directly in the hands of business people.

> Business Process Management (BPM) is what sets "enterprise cloud computing" apart from "consumer cloud computing."

What's a business process? As clearly defined in the seminal book, *Business Process Management: The Third Wave*, "A business process is the complete set of transactional and collaborative activities that bring value to customers." Unique business processes are how companies differentiate themselves, and are thus paramount to the enterprise use of cloud computing.

> Because the typical end-to-end business process involves over 20 companies in any given value chain, *multi-company* BPM is essential to gaining and maintaining competitive advantage.
>
> Bringing BPM capabilities to the Cloud enables multiple companies to share a common BPM environment and fully participate in an overall end-to-end business process.

BPMaaS covers the full lifecycle of business processes, from their conception, design, implementation and ongoing optimization. We devote a later chapter to this critical component of enterprise cloud computing, with an emphasis on "on-demand" business processes.

BPMaaS may be implemented as a form of Business Process Outsourcing (BPO) with the functionality centered on a particular industry. Such "vertical" implementations would embody specific vocabularies, master data management and core business processes unique to a given industry. Such implementations would most likely be carried out in Community Clouds where a group of companies share a group firewall.

On the other hand, BPMaaS can be implemented as a "horizontal" Business Operations Platform (BOP) that has a Business Process Management System (BPMS) at its heart. This is similar to PaaS, but rather than programming tools being accessed, the BPMS is being accessed for full process lifecycle management and specific process services such as process modeling and business activity monitoring (BAM).

- 5. *Management Controls as a Service (MCaaS)*. MCaaS offers services such as monitoring service-level agreements with Cloud providers, security management, distributed policy management, role-based authentication and authorization, and other foundation services needed by all layers in the Cloud stack. The lower down the Software-Platform-Infrastructure (SPI) stack the more security and other capabilities consumers are responsible for implementing and managing themselves. On the other hand, the further up the stack, the less the consumer needs be concerned about how each of the lower levels works. Regardless of where the consumer participates in the stack, management controls are essential no matter who has the responsibility, the consumer or the Cloud Service Provider (CSP).

One of the most difficult aspects of governance to get right in the Cloud are the lines of responsibility and escalation procedures. In a traditional, centralized "command and control" IT architecture, it's relatively easy to establish lines of responsibility and to create escalation procedures to accommodate situations that go wrong. In a Cloud environment, this model needs to be re-thought. If a service is run by a third party, then what happens in the event of an outage? A given service may be a crucial component of a multi-company process. How will the cause of the problem be identified and who will be responsible to expedite the solution? For example, if a "customer credit check" service becomes unavailable or unacceptably slow, then multiple other processes that have a dependency on the service, such as quoting, order entry, shipping and invoicing, will be adversely impacted.

Here are some more significant headaches calling for MCaaS:
— How does an individual or group of individuals plan to supply a service when they have no way of predicting how many people will access the service and when?
— How can they manage a process where multiple companies are collaborating, but nobody is necessarily in charge?
— Who ensures that the overall service being delivered is secure, reliable and available?

These governance challenges are critically important to address, but they should not deter moving to a Cloud model— they are solvable, and the benefits of collaboration between organizations provide extensive benefits to the business.

As is the case with the common characteristic of cloud computing to be *autonomic* (a system that operates and serves its purpose by managing itself without external intervention even in case of environmental changes), governance too must involve distributed policy management that conforms to "autonomic self-properties:" self-configuration, self-healing, self-optimization and self-protection. The days of inside-out, centralized "command and control" IT architecture and governance are over. MCaaS is needed at every level in the Cloud stack.

Policy management for the Cloud environment is very much still in its infancy, but right now is the time to get some principles in place. In their book, *Lost in Translation*, Carl Bate and Nigel Green define "a service" (meaning an individual service corresponding to a business task) around five principles that provide a useful starting point. The key is to first define the granularity (the business detail) of the service with respect to the business task which they call its "Value" statement, and this also provides the registry name for the service itself. The remaining four characteristics are "Policy" – meaning what policies need to be applied to this service; "Events" – which events are involved; "Content" – created or consumed; and "Trust" – who can do what. Following the VPEC-T approach means, from the very beginning, building up the correct sort of policies using the creation of the new environment as the focus to determine what sort of policies are needed.

It actually gets better than that because the Content, Events, and Trust relationships should also be mapped, thus creating from the very beginning a reasonable governance structure for maintaining services. If you change a policy, clearly you will know which services will be affected, and from that which processes the service appears in, and therefore the impact. The same holds true for Content, Events, or even Trust; it's a pretty self evident way of getting a grip on what will turn into a huge problem very quickly as the number of services rapidly multiply.

Take all these considerations into account, add in the requirements for Cloud portability and interoperability, and the expertise and skills in a typical enterprise can become overwhelmed. Hence the rise of specialty firms, Cloud Brokerages. Gartner outlined three categories of opportunities for Cloud brokers:

1. Cloud Service Intermediation Brokers: Building services atop an existing cloud platform, such as additional security or management capabilities.

2. Aggregation Brokers: Deploying customer services over multiple cloud platforms.

3. Cloud Service Arbitrage: Brokers supply flexibility and "opportunistic choices" and foster competition between Clouds.

"The future of cloud computing will be permeated with the notion of brokers negotiating relationships between providers of cloud services and the service customers," Gartner analyst L. Frank Kenney said in a statement. "In this context, a broker might be software, appliances, platforms or suites of technologies that enhance the base services available through the Cloud. Enhancement will include managing access to these services, providing greater security or even creating completely new services."

As cited in an *eWeek* report,[3] "Gartner analysts see three different types of CSBs (cloud service brokerages) arising, the first being a cloud service intermediation broker. Brokers will add value on top of the services being delivered, with those services including identity management and access management. The brokers and their products will be found in the Cloud at the service provider's location, at the user's location or in the Cloud as a service.

"Aggregation brokers will be used to combine multiple services into one or more new services, taking the burden of data integration, process integrity or intermediation off the end user, according to Gartner. The aggregation broker will ensure the integration, movement and security of the data between the user and providers. These brokers will live primarily in the Cloud, the analysts said. The services that aggregation brokerages offer will be fixed, with little or no changes.

"Finally, Cloud service arbitrage will be similar to Cloud service aggregation, except that the services being aggregated won't be fixed. That flexibility will be important, Gartner analysts said, doing such chores as providing multiple e-mail services through one service provider or providing a credit-scoring service that checks multiple scoring agencies, then selects the best score.

"'What sits between you and the Cloud will become a critical success factor in cloud computing as Cloud services multiply and expand faster than the ability of Cloud consumers to manage or govern them in use,' Gartner analyst Daryl Plummer said in a statement. 'The growth of service brokerage businesses will increase the ability of Cloud consumers to use services in a trustworthy manner. Cloud service providers must begin to partner with cloud brokerages to ensure that they can deliver the services they promote.'"

Eli Lilly uses Cloud services providers to tap high-performance computing for hundreds of its scientists, and a 64-node Linux cluster can be online in five minutes, compared with three months internally. But looking ahead, Eli Lilly wants to head off a scenario where it has to configure and manage each Cloud service separately. The company wants a "brokerage" layer that sits between it and the various Cloud services it wants to use. That layer would determine the best Cloud service for a particular job based on cost and performance. Eli Lilly also talks about the potential to use cloud computing for external collaboration and envisions going to the point where the Cloud becomes a point of integration among external researchers.

While security is popularly stated as the biggest cloud computing concern, the technical issues are tractable. Processes and techniques for the management of security and associated risks are typically organizational policy and operational decisions. According to Cloud computing practitioner and pioneer, Kevin Jackson, "The most important barrier to wholesale expansion and adoption of enterprise-class cloud computing is interoperability and portability. It is indeed this concern that has led to the creation of the Cloud brokerage industry."

Deployment Models
- *Private cloud.* The cloud infrastructure is operated solely for an organization. It may be managed by the organization or a third party and may exist on premise or off premise (a Virtual Private Cloud or VPC).
- *Community cloud.* The cloud infrastructure is shared by several

organizations and supports a specific community that has shared concerns (e.g., mission, security requirements, policy, and compliance considerations). It may be managed by the organizations or a third party and may exist on premise or off premise.

- *Public cloud.* The cloud infrastructure is made available to the general public or a large industry group and is owned by an organization selling cloud services.

- *Hybrid cloud.* The cloud infrastructure is a composition of two or more clouds (private, community, or public) that remain unique entities but are bound together by standardized or proprietary technology that enables data and application portability (e.g., cloud bursting).

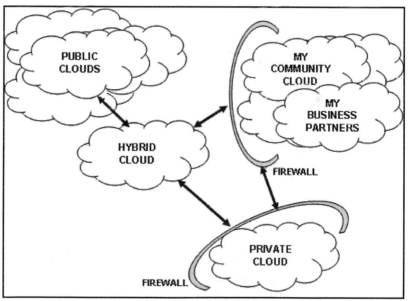

Cloud Computing Deployment Models

Each deployment model instance has one of two types, internal or external. Internal clouds reside within an organizations network security perimeter and external clouds reside outside the same perimeter.

With regard to Private Clouds, George Barlow, CEO of Cloud Harbor, points out a sometimes overlooked aspect of private clouds, "Few people yet understand the major role enterprise software appliances will play in the upcoming cloud computing revolution. Appliance-based Software Delivery (AbSD) is an emerging technology that puts ready-to-run applications on a server (appliance) that is built specifically to be deployed on-premise, behind the firewall of an enterprise computing installation. These appliances will contain the same applications that run on servers in the cloud and be maintained exclusively by the cloud application vendors at the same application release level as the corresponding cloud offerings. The main advantage of AbSD applications is that they are securely connected to both the Cloud and the organization's on-premise networks. This affords the enterprise the safety and convenience of keeping data and connections to existing on-premise applications behind the organization's firewall while still allowing most of the advantages of the Software-as-a-Service (SaaS) or Platform-as-a-Service (PaaS) computing model."

In summary, while the basic technologies of cloud computing have been available for some time, a wide array of IT resources and, more importantly, business "services" can now be allocated and consumed *on demand* without the consumers having to deal with the underlying details and complexities.

So it is that it's the *delivery* of IT and business services that has changed, changed utterly. In these days where a company depends on technology for its operations and its innovation capabilities, the enterprise itself will be changed, changed utterly.

Why Is Cloud Computing So Hard To Understand?

Why is cloud computing so hard to understand? It would be an equally fair question to ask why today's Information Technology is so hard to understand. The answer would be because it covers the entire range of business requirements, from back office enterprise systems to various ways such systems can be implemented. Cloud computing covers an equal breadth of both technology and, equally important, business requirements. Therefore many different definitions are acceptable and fall within the overall topic.

But why use the term "cloud computing" at all? It originates from the work to develop easy-to-use Consumer IT (Web 2.0) and its differences from existing difficult-to-use enterprise IT systems. A Web 2.0 site allows its users to interact with other users or to change content, in contrast to non-interactive Web 1.0 sites where users are limited to the passive viewing of information that is provided to them. Although the term Web 2.0 suggests a new version of the World Wide Web, it does *not* refer to new technology, but rather to cumulative changes in the ways software developers and end-users *use* the Web. World Wide Web inventor Tim Berners-Lee clarifies, "I think Web 2.0 is, of course, a piece of jargon, nobody even knows what it means. If Web 2.0 for you is blogs and wikis, then that is 'people to people.' But that was what the Web was supposed to be all along. The Web was designed to be a collaborative space where people can interact." In short, Web 2.0 isn't new technology; it's an emerging usage pattern. Ditto for cloud computing; it's an emerging usage pattern that draws on existing forms of IT resources.

Extending Berners-Lee's definition of Web 2.0, the companion to this book, *Dot Cloud: The 21st Century Business Platform*, helps clarify that cloud computing isn't a new technology, "The Cloud is the 'real Internet' or what the Internet was really meant to be in the first place, an endless computer made up of networks of networks of computers. For geeks, cloud computing has been used to mean grid computing, utility computing, software as a service, virtualization, Internet-based applications, autonomic computing, peer-to-peer computing and remote processing—and various combinations of these terms. For non-geeks, cloud computing is simply a platform where individuals and companies use the internet to access endless hardware software and data resources for most of their computing needs and people-to-people interactions, leaving the mess to third party suppliers."

> Again, cloud computing isn't new technology;
> it's a newly evolved *delivery* model.

The key point is that cloud computing focuses on the end users and their abilities to do what they want to do, singularly or in communities, without the need for specialized IT support. The technology layer is *abstracted*, or hidden, and is simply represented by a drawing of a "Cloud." This same principle has been used in the past for certain technologies such as the Internet itself.

At the same time as the Web 2.0 technologists were perfecting their approach to *people-centric* collaboration, interactions, use of search and so on, traditional IT technologists were working to improve the flexibility and usability of existing IT resources. This was the path that led to *virtualization*, the ability to share computational resources and reduce the barriers of costs and overhead of system administration. Flexibility in computational resources was in fact exactly what was needed to support the Web 2.0 environment. Whereas IT was largely based on a known and limited number of users working on a known and limited number of applications, Web 2.0 is based on any number of users deploying any number of services, as and when required in a totally random dynamic demand model.

The trend toward improving the cost and flexibility of current in-house IT capabilities by using virtualization can be said to be a part of cloud computing as much as shifting to Web-based applications supplied as services from a specialist online provider. Thus it is helpful to define cloud computing in terms of usage patterns or "use cases" for internal cost savings or external human collaboration more than defining the technical aspects.

There are differences in regional emphases on what is driving the adoption of cloud computing. The North American market is more heavily focused on a new wave of IT system upgrades; the European market is more focused on the delivery of new marketplaces and services; and the Asian market is more focused on the ability to jump past on-premise IT and go straight to remote service centers.

There is a real shift in business requirements that is driving the "use" as a defining issue. IT has done its work of automating back office business processes and improving enterprise efficiency very well, so well that studies show the percentage of an office worker's time spent on processes has dropped steadily. Put another way, the routine elements of operations have been identified and optimized.

But now it's the front office activities of interacting with customers, suppliers and trading partners that make up the majority of the work. Traditional IT has done little to address this as its core technologies and methodologies of tightly-coupled, data-centric applications simply aren't suitable for the user-driven flexibility that is required in the front office. The needed technology shift can be summarized as one from "supply push" to "demand pull" of data, information and services.

Business requirements are increasingly being focused on the front office around improving revenues, margins, market share, and customer services. To address these requirements a change in the core technologies is needed in order to deliver diversity around the *edge* of the business where differentiation and real revenue value are created. Web 2.0 user-centric capabilities are seen as a significant part of the answer. The technology model of flexible combinations of "services" instead of monolithic applications, combined with user-driven orchestration of those services, supports this shifting front office emphasis on the use of technology in business.

It's not even just a technology and requirement match; it's also a match on the supply side. These new Web 2.0 requirements delivered through the Cloud offer fast, even instantaneous, implementations with no capital cost or provisioning time. This contrasts to the yearly budget and cost recovery models of traditional back office IT. In fact many Cloud-based front office services may only have a life of a few weeks or months as business needs continually change to suit the increasingly dynamic nature of global markets. Thus the supply of pay-as-you-go instant provisioning of resources is a core driver in the adoption of cloud computing. This funding model of direct cost attribution to the business user is in stark contrast to the traditional overhead recovery IT model.

While cloud computing can reduce the cost and complexity of provisioning computational capabilities, it also can be used to build new shared service centers operating with greater effectiveness "at the edge" of the business where there's money to be made. Front office requirements focus on people, expertise, and collaboration in any-to-any combinations.

> Back-office IT is for after-the-fact recordkeeping.
> Front-office IT is for *conducting* business in real time.

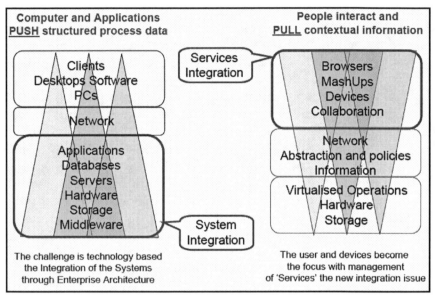

Technology Shift from Push to Pull

Returning to the book, *Dot.Cloud*, "There will be many ways in which the Cloud will change businesses and the economy, most of them hard to predict, but one theme is already emerging. Businesses are becoming more like the technology itself: more adaptable, more interwoven and more specialized. These developments may not be new, but the advent of cloud computing will speed them up."

Enterprise Use Case Scenarios

A set of useful cloud computing usage scenarios were posited in a white paper produced by the Cloud Computing Use Case Discussion Group. According to the group, these Enterprise Cloud Usage scenarios are intended to illustrate the most typical Cloud use cases and are not meant to be an exhaustive list of realizations within a Cloud environment.

- *End User to Cloud:* Applications running on the cloud and accessed by end users
- *Enterprise to Cloud to End User:* Applications running in the public Cloud and accessed by employees and customers
- *Enterprise to Cloud:* Cloud applications integrated with internal IT capabilities
- *Enterprise to Cloud to Enterprise:* Cloud applications running in the public cloud and interoperating with partner applications (e.g., supply chain partners)
- *Private Cloud:* A cloud hosted by an organization inside that organization's firewall.
- *Changing Cloud Vendors:* An organization using Cloud services decides to switch Cloud providers or work with additional providers.
- *Hybrid Cloud:* Multiple Clouds work together, often coordinated by a cloud broker that federates data, applications, user identity, security and other details.

For a detailed discussion of these use cases, see Appendix A.

Additional Background Concepts

The main ideas behind cloud computing aren't new. They go way back to the 1960s with the advent of "timesharing" (multitenancy) where companies like GTE, IBM (The Service Bureau) and GE entered the business of offering the power of massive mainframe computers as a service to others that could ill afford such raw computing power. Companies such as GTE Data Services offered standard packaged computer applications for financial institutions under the billing model of a "computer utility."

But the advent of the minicomputer in the 1970s along with a recession squelched these new computing services models.

Fast forward to the 21st century. Instead of sharing mainframe computing capacity, the Cloud is all about sharing massive server farms made up of commodity PCs. Sometimes these come in the form of public Cloud offerings. At other times they are virtual computing "software appliances" that provide cloud computing inside a given company's firewall.

In reflection, advances in computing and delivery models didn't die away. During the dot-com boom the application service provider (ASP) emerged. Simultaneously, other delivery models rose up such as grid computing for high performance processing power, co-location for resource sharing, and on-demand computing, to name a few.

Most recognizable among these models, especially as it relates to cloud computing, is the Software as a Service Model (SaaS). The first company that comes to mind with the SaaS model is Salesforec.com with its customer relationship management system (CRM) used by thousands of companies. SaaS is much like on-premise software for CRM, or enterprise resource planning (ERP) or supply chain management (SCM) but hosted off premises and delivered via the Web. SaaS is certainly a part of "the Cloud," but there's much more, and it's clear why Salesforce.com has moved on to Force.com. And new entrants such as Cordys with its Business Operations Platform are gaining significant uptake as they offer Business Process Management (BPMaaS). Here's why.

When most people think of SaaS, they think of familiar software from the on-premise world, such as CRM, ERP or personal productivity packages, and imagine the same applications delivered over the Web. During the dot-com era this was the model used by Application Service Providers (ASPs). Due to their monolithic and inflexible applications, the ASPs went the way of the dot-com bust. In his blog entry, *Thinking Beyond SaaS As We Know It,* analyst Phil Wainewright describes an example of going beyond. Phil writes, "ServiceChannel, helps large companies manage relationships with local suppliers of cleaning, maintenance and other services. National chains need someone to service their local stores and usually hire a local small business to do things like check the plumbing or clean the storefront glass. This is an area of mind-numbingly wasteful administrative activity that's truly ripe for automation. ServiceChannel's software automates processes around hiring and credentialing contractors, managing and validating the work as it's done, and then approving and paying invoices. It allows for compliance with Sarbanes-Oxley regulations and can integrate into

ERP systems including Oracle and SAP." [4]

Why Phil likes this example is that it's more than just an application; it's a complete solution to a pain point for many businesses. Both large chains are targeted as buyers and also the small businesses that act as their local contractors. It solves the problem by bringing together not only software, but also a network infrastructure using the Web to connect businesses that are currently wasting huge amounts of energy and time on manual processes. Once it gains momentum, it has the potential to also act as a marketplace in which local contractors can offer their services to branches of several different chains.

With the Cloud we can now envision a rich ecosystem of services among businesses and individuals that delivers information where, when and how it's needed. According to Russ Daniels, V.P. and chief technology officer of Cloud Services Strategy at Hewlett-Packard, "This is truly just the beginning. The cloud makes it possible to deliver everything as a service—from business processes to personal interactions—and to create altogether new business models across industries." [5]

A Cloud in every startup garage? Stay tuned.

Gartner analyst, Daryl Plummer commented, "Russ gets at the point that while use of standard virtualized technology underlies the concept of cloud computing, the real value comes from all of us seeking to use shared cloud services on massively shared and standard public cloud infrastructure to gain economic and efficiency advantages while refocusing most of our attention on our core-competencies. He uses the automobile industry as an example of how mass-production, standardization, and entrepreneurship can be used to grow business and to create new capabilities for those who need them. He says it all in the following quote: 'In my view, the ability to facilitate innovation and entrepreneurship in this new model is one of the most promising ways to ignite the next wave of economic growth. We can no more see the full impact of the cloud than Henry Ford foresaw the impact of his desire to produce more cars in less time.'" [6] We might add to Plummer's observation that Ford also introduced the standardization of parts, making ongoing maintenance and operational costs far less. Such standardization also plays a key role in cloud computing.

What the Cloud really represents is the knee in an exponential growth curve, the next stage in the evolution of the Internet. It's what the Internet was really meant to be in the first place—an endless computer made up of networks of networks of computers. Notions of time-sharing, computer utilities and "the network is the computer" (as Sun Microsystems' John Gage declared in 1984) have been around for quite some time. Unfortunately, early visions were constrained by a lack of network bandwidth. But now that the overabundance of dark fiber laid down during the dot-com boom is being lit up, it's time for a "computer utility redux" in the form of cloud computing.

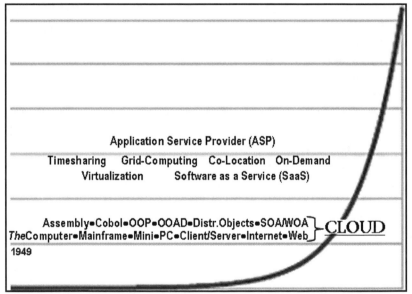

The Cloud Represents the Knee in an Exponential Growth Curve

Of course the future won't be just the sum of technologies past. Just as each technology advancement has required new technology architectures (from monolithic programs, to objects, to n-tier client-server technologies) Service-oriented architecture (SOA) is key to cloud computing. Companies will need to refactor in-side-out application architectures for governing access and security policies while embracing the outside-in architectural style of SOA for distributed services. This architectural transition is crucial for successful migration to enterprise-class cloud computing.

So it seems that cloud computing, despite all the hype, isn't new at all. That is, it's built on and leverages established technologies. So what's the big deal?

As Boston Consulting Group's George Stalk writes in *Five Future Strategies You Need Right Now (Memo to the CEO)*, "We're not there yet, but it won't be long before we live in a world where companies can effortlessly receive any amount of information they want, in any form they need, at any time and place, and at zero cost. When that world materializes (or perhaps I should say dematerializes), some companies will be ready to take advantage of their newfound power and capability, others will not. There are three important areas in which infinite bandwidth can create competitive advantage: increasing operational efficiencies, creating new business models, and establishing whole new businesses. These issues may still seem to be faint signals to you. But like so many emerging issues of the past fifty years, these are likely to appear on the front pages of the business press before you know it."

Cloud computing builds on established technologies to drive down the cost of the *delivery* of services while increasing the speed and agility with which services are deployed. As Sun Microsystems wrote in one of its white papers, "It shortens the time from sketching out an application architecture to actual deployment. Cloud computing incorporates virtualization, on-demand deployment, Internet delivery of services, and open source software. From one perspective, cloud computing is nothing new because it uses approaches, concepts, and best practices that have already been established. From another perspective, everything is new because cloud computing changes how we invent, develop, deploy, scale, update, maintain, and pay for applications and the infrastructure on which they run."

What makes the Cloud real is the maturation of the Internet as a platform, reliable virtualization, commoditization and the introduction of various standards. A recent analysis of cloud computing in *The Economist* [7] stated that there are a plethora of data centers worldwide, with an estimated 7,000 data centers in America alone. Most of these data centers are one-off designs that have grown over the years. Many surveys show that these data centers are highly inefficient. According to a study by consultancy McKinsey and the think-tank, Uptime Institute, on average only 6% of server capacity is used. Nearly 30% of servers are no longer in use at all and many organizations are unaware of which application is running on which server. What a waste and just think of the impact on the environment.

According to IDC a quarter of corporate data centers in America have run out of space for more servers. For others, cooling has become a big constraint and often utility providers cannot supply the extra power required for an expansion. Increasingly all of these factors will be overtaken by the green legal requirements —in short, companies will have to change. IDC believes that many data centers will have to be consolidated and overhauled. Hewlett-Packard used to have 85 data centers with 19,000 IT workers worldwide, but is expected to reduce this down to six facilities in America with just 8,000 employees, reducing its IT budget from 4% to 2% of revenue by embracing private Clouds. HP is not alone as companies strive to become more efficient in a world of extreme competition.

This Cloud of computing resources will not only affect the number of data centers and the number of people employed in them, it will have profound implications for the organization. On one level the Cloud will be a huge collection of electronic services based on standards. Many Web-based services are built to be integrated into existing business processes, allowing organizations to become more modular, flexible, and specialized. In the Cloud it will become even easier to outsource business processes, or at least those parts where companies do not enjoy a competitive advantage. This also means that organizations will rely more on services provided by others.

Furthermore, there will be not just one Cloud but a number of different Clouds, both private and public, which themselves will divide into general-purpose and specialized Clouds. People are already using the term "InterCloud" to mean a federation of all kinds of Clouds, in the same way that the Internet is a network of networks. All of those Clouds will be full of applications and services.

Thanks to the availability of bandwidth, the Internet becomes the access point to powerful, preexisting technologies that huge enterprises and individuals alike can use without having to house them, manage them, provision them—or buy them. The range of available services starts with simple things like free email and goes all the way to Web-scale supercomputing resources.

> The key is *elastic scalability*;
> use as much or as little as needed in a given situation.

"During the past 15 years, a continuing trend toward IT industrialization has grown in popularity as IT services have become repeatable and usable by a wide range of customers," highlights Gartner's Daryl Plummer. "This is due, in part to the commoditization and standardization of technologies, in part to virtualization and the rise of service-oriented software architectures, and most importantly, to the dramatic growth in popularity of the Internet."

What does cloud computing mean to IT? Plummer continues by stating that taken together, these three major trends constitute the basis of a discontinuity that will create a new opportunity to shape the relationship between those who use IT services and those who sell them.

Returning to Russ Daniels at HP, "Something profound is occurring, something that will extend the reach of information technology to vast new markets, increase its value to existing ones and change the structure of the IT industry." He goes on to say in his blog, "Cloud services enable businesses to create richer, deeper relationships with customers, to treat each one as an individual, to customize offerings to meet the specific needs of each, and to integrate with the business partners to make this happen smoothly, and affordably." We might also add, the Cloud opens up on-demand well-defined, compliant business processes.

There will be an ever diminishing requirement for business users to fund the purchase and deployment of large enterprise applications. They will use specific services to do specific tasks as and when required for unique situations. As highlighted below, the key mechanisms for delivering these services are business process management (BPM) techniques (we discuss BPM in more detail later in this book). As stated in *Dot Cloud: The 21st Century Business Platform* it's only a matter of time before IT roles change, "The forward-thinking CIO will no doubt put his or her head in the Clouds and change his or her title to Chief Process Officer (CPO), for it's agile business processes that companies want to manage, not technology infrastructures."

Now if this discussion has favored painting the Cloud as a source of IT cost savings, think again. While elastic scalability, up or down, is an obvious cost-saving benefit of cloud computing, the true significance isn't about *cost savings*, it's about:

- Taking *collaboration* (both human collaboration and business process collaboration) to a new level among individuals and companies.
- Sharing a common *information and computational base* among individuals and companies.
- *Collective intelligence* and the wisdom of crowds.

> The deeper business benefits of the Cloud add up to
> *business innovation* on demand.

The Larger Economic Context: The Perfect Storm

The global economic crisis that began in 2008 was created by a perfect storm of mutually reinforcing trends and policy mistakes. It would be the first time there had been an overall contraction in developed economies since World War II. It's not at all clear which direction organizations will be pushed in, but they do not have to be passive onlookers while unexpected change continues to come their way.

We all know the economic horror stories that began making headlines starting in 2008, but something else was in the air, something really big. In his book, *Beyond the Crisis: The Future of Capitalism*, renowned Dutch futurologist, Adjiedj Bakas, wrote, "The Chinese phrase for crisis consists of two words *danger* and *opportunity*. The crash of 2008 was the fifth major crisis in 200 years. All of them occurred at the transition from one era to the next. The 1930s may have been a time of deep economic crisis and mass unemployment, yet in those days the Kennedy's made their fortunes, art deco was born and the radio, car, and telephone grew to be so much in demand that great new industries emerged out of the ashes of the crisis. During the current crisis we finally say goodbye to the 20th century and transit into a new era with new economic pillars and digital collaboration powered by cloud computing. This transition period offers tremendous opportunities."

Harvard's Lynda Applegate elaborates on the role of innovation in uncertain economic times, "Some people think about innovation and new ventures as a side business to running the real business, but the economic downturn takes the need for innovation to a new level. In this environment, 'business as usual' is not the answer. One of the things we know is that the interest in innovation is being spurred by radical change and disruption that is going on in the business environment. Companies must work aggressively to innovate and make the kinds of changes that are critical to success today and in the years to come. They must consider cost cutting as just one step on the journey to future success. In a sense, every business, large or small, needs to think of itself as a 'new venture' right now. This is a time of unprecedented opportunity to rethink offerings, markets, business processes, and organizational structure—and to improve them to achieve growth. Entrepreneurs view threats as opportunities, and innovation is the relentless pursuit of new opportunities regardless of the resources at your disposal."[8]

To make such *rethinking* actionable, the focus must not be on *what* you do, but *how* you do what you do, and that's about your business processes. Even more it's about weaving a tapestry of end-to-end business processes that span *multiple* companies in a typical value delivery system. Changing offerings, reaching new markets, changing organizational structure and innovation itself are all about business processes (*how* you do what you do), and a business operations platform in the Cloud can offer unbounded resources that are within reach of even the smallest company.

With business process innovation capabilities in hand, a company can go after a greater share of existing customers' wallets instead of just seeking greater market share for existing products and services. Companies can extend their product offerings with services offerings as IBM has done. 70% of IBM's total revenues now comes from services. Virgin Atlantic is in the bridal clothing business, grabbing a greater share of its airline customers' wallets. Walmart is in the health clinic and banking businesses. Exxon is in the coffee business. UPS is in the computer repair business. Starbucks is in the music business. All of these companies are going after a greater share of their customers' wallets.

Amazon is in the computing business. Out of nowhere Animoto has created a brand new market that didn't exist before. Animoto lets the masses, businesses and educators turn photos into artsy MTV-like music videos using artificial intelligence. When it launched on Facebook demand was such that it had to increase the number of its virtual machines on Amazon's EC2 (Elastic Compute Cloud) from a handful to thousands within six days. Nowhere else could that on-demand business innovation happen except in the elastic Cloud.

In addition to extending a company's offerings for its existing markets, it's easier than ever to reach emerging markets and to streamline processes through outsourcing and forming partnerships in the global marketplace. As former Reuters CIO Ken Thompson reports in his book, *The Networked Enterprise*, Europe leads the way in smaller companies coming together to form *virtual enterprise networks* to compete with the power of the big fish across multiple industries.

Opportunities abound, and to paraphrase Alan Kay, a pioneer at Xerox PARC, from the 1968 Dynabook project that ultimately led to the Macintosh PC, "If the mind can conceive it, the Cloud can be used to achieve it." Let the Cloud-empowered innovation games begin!

Takeaway

"When it comes to the future, there are three kinds of people: those who let it happen, those who make it happen, and those who wonder what happened."—John M. Richardson, Jr.

Organizations should use the Perfect Storm as an opportunity to get fit and healthy. There is an idiom that states "a better built ship can weather a storm." An organization should take a good look at what it does but most importantly it should take a long hard look at *how* it does things.

Cloud computing can provide powerful business benefits to companies. The late management sage Peter Drucker once said, "Time is the scarcest resource." For many companies, by the time new hardware and software can be specified, procured and implemented, the business opportunity has passed and the value is lost. With the Cloud, this risk is eliminated because many of these elements can be accessed immediately as services. This is especially important as the outlook for business suggests more frequent changes in both its external products as well as its internal systems in increasingly competitive global markets.

As a final point let's turn the clock back ten years when the world was obsessed with the Y2K problem at the turn of the century. It is unclear exactly how much was spent on IT to ensure a successful transition into the Millennium – although an estimate of around $200 billion sounds plausible. While organizations were checking millions of lines of code, two students took another look at an everyday problem. The students focused on how searching across the Internet worked and could work much better. The students came up with an elegant solution and Google was born. The rest is history.

References.

[1]

   http://www.google.com/a/help/intl/en/admins/pdf/forrester_cloud_em
ail_cost_analysis.pdf

[2] Adapted from NIST Presentation:
   http://www.csrc.nist.gov/groups/SNS/cloud-computing/index.html

[3] http://www.eweek.com/c/a/Cloud-Computing/Gartner-Predict-Rise-of-
Cloud-Service-Brokerages-759833/

[4]

   http://www.ebizq.net/blogs/connectedweb/2009/07/thinking_beyond_s
aas_as_we_kno.php?mkt_tok=3RkMMJWWfF9wsRonsqzfLqzsmxzEJ8rw
7u8rT%2Frn28M3109ad%2BrmPBy934I%3D

[5] http://www.forbes.com/2009/05/07/cloud-computing-enterprise-
technology-cio-network-cloud-computing_print.html

[6] http://blogs.gartner.com/daryl_plummer/

[7] Let it Rise. A special report on corporate IT. 25th October 2008.

[8] http://hbswk.hbs.edu/item/6159.html

3. Welcome to the Human Network

"When technology meets humanity on the human network,
the way we work changes. The way we live changes. Everything
changes. That's the human network effect." [1]
—Cisco Systems

"Something is happening, but you don't know what it is, do you,
Mister Jones?"
—Bob Dylan, *"Ballad of a Thin Man"*

Key Points: The Connected Society is Changing How Businesses Operate

No, this chapter isn't an advertisement about Cisco Systems, Inc., but we can thank Cisco for the "Human Network" phrase that puts in a nutshell what's going on in our wired world.

Indeed, "Something is happening, but you don't know what it is, do you, Mister Jones?" And *that something* is really big. Thus we devote a rather big chapter to exploring that something from multiple perspectives.

Technology has always changed the affairs of humans: the wheel, agriculture, printing press, steam engine, railroads, modern medicine, radio and television. In recent times it's been the telecommunication network and then the computer network. But now, it's the *human network* where we go beyond the use of electromagnetic energy to connect with machines and data and on to connecting humans in ways never before so practical.

Before we can properly discuss the changing role of information technology in business, we need to set the context of what's happening in the larger world *outside* business, in our hyperconnected society, as a result of dramatic advances brought about by the Internet. The bottom line?

> It's not about the real-time enterprise;
> It's about the real-time society
> where people and events constantly interact and organize
> their personal and community ecosystems.

Author Yochai Benkler makes a very interesting observation, "That the Internet is changing society is understood. Less appreciated is how society is changing the Internet." People are becoming the resource, a resource that's even more powerful than CPU cycles and database resources.

We don't connect to the Web just to connect to data and facts. We connect to connect with people for both the content and context they provide. Welcome to the Human Network.

Okay, we won't re-explain what you already know: Innovation, not land, labor and capital, is now the secret sauce of competitive advantage.

"Modern economies," *The Economist* recently noted, "are not built with capital or labor as much as by ideas." By some estimates nearly half America's gross domestic product is based on intellectual property. As the knowledge economy rapidly morphs into the creative economy, it's becoming more urgent than ever to understand creativity, especially those leaps that change the very nature of the game.

Of course those leaps that change the game are what companies desperately seek in the creative economy. Leading companies are turning to Social Networks to tap new sources of business intelligence and creativity that can lead to innovation. Yet others view Social Networks as some newfangled time waster and a distraction. It's likely that the word "social" in Social Networking has puzzled business managers. After all, Social Networks aren't new, and here's perhaps what your boss thinks of them, a digital version of Woodstock, 1969:

Woodstock, 1969

The abundance of social media is creating an overabundance of noise. So of course your boss is not the least bit interested in having employees take up such time wasters.

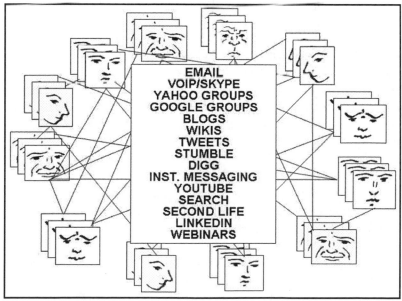

EMAIL
VOIP/SKYPE
YAHOO GROUPS
GOOGLE GROUPS
BLOGS
WIKIS
TWEETS
STUMBLE
DIGG
INST. MESSAGING
YOUTUBE
SEARCH
SECOND LIFE
LINKEDIN
WEBINARS

Social Networks Equal Noise

In a nutshell, Social Networking is a two-edged sword, as both a real time waster and a new source of business intelligence. Because it's easier than ever to reach a large audience, but harder than ever to really connect with it, companies will have to think long and hard about Social Networking if they are to gain the potential benefits. So, let's explore some of the many aspects of Social Networks as they can and probably will impact the enterprise.

Being In the Know

The ability of people to actively use their individual and collective expertise to respond to events is at the core of Social Networking. That term conjures up as much confusion as cloud computing as it implies that it has little or nothing to do with business or work and everything to do with an individual's social life. The term actually reflects the human trait of socializing or sharing experiences, knowledge and expertise in a dynamic and adaptive manner, as distinct from traditional knowledge management which relates to the collection and collation of static facts.

For businesses and governments the challenge is how to participate and perform in this new world of Social Networking against revised expectations. Expertise and services are the most difficult commodities to track as they flow across state and national boundaries. This together with an open society adds to the challenges of businesses and governments. Think of it as the biggest advent in democracy since printing enabled political pamphlets allowing the formation of political parties that could communicate their ideas reliably.

Personal and collective expertise is at a premium to live successfully, and more and more we are all forced to compete online for our roles at work and in society. Furthermore, we are witnessing the transition of the notion of "intelligence" from "knowledge" to "knowing."

Traditional business intelligence (BI) has really meant internal intelligence on how well the enterprise is performing against the targets it had set for itself. But the real challenge is how to gain external intelligence about current events and opportunities in order to make quality business decisions and boost performance.

That's *not* so easy if you really break it down into practical steps.

After all, we don't know what we don't know, so we have no way of knowing how complete a picture we are using to inform our decisions. Think of it this way. You're hungry (event), and see what looks like a good restaurant (opportunity). Then you study the menu (knowledge), and subsequently decide to eat there (decision). The food is okay, but the evening is not great as you are lonely, so the experience is poor (optimization).

Now add Twitter, which is up to a staggering number of users, into the equation. Our friends are offering continual insights into their activities so now we have the benefit of "knowing" more about the whole experience. We could ask for feedback on the restaurant, or for recommendations on other restaurants nearby. We could even see that we have a friend nearby with whom we could share the meal. We could thus describe ourselves as being "in the know" – a unique English phrase used to describe people who always seems to have connections and experiences that give them an edge over most other people.

Is enabling us to feel that we are "in the know" the secret of Twitter's success? And can that experience be replicated across an enterprise through social networking tools? Can we progress from what we think of as traditional pre-ordained "knowledge" to "knowing?" This shift is a fundamental concept for business intelligence in the Internet age.

The notion of knowledge versus knowing has been aired in a number of different ways ranging from spiritual issues to the sciences, as discussed in an interesting book, *Knowing Knowledge*, by George Siemens. In an informative review of the book, Marjorie Desgrosseilliers wrote, "According to Siemens, knowing and learning take place much the same way today. Knowledge is born through building concept upon concept, mixed with pieces taken from various and often chaotic sources. Knowledge comes and is defined through connections not necessarily aligned in a predefined, linear format. Knowledge is no longer shaped by categorization and disseminated through hierarchies.

"A major change occurred as we moved from the industrial age into the information age: instead of one-way learning, we want a two-way street to engage in and reshape the knowledge we find. We want to connect with others to learn what they know, and then make that knowledge our own (blogs, wikis, etc). According to Siemens, doing so diminishes the 'prominence of the originator.' Knowledge doesn't come solely through static products (books or lesson plans created years before publishing). With the advent of the Internet and Web 2.0 technologies, knowledge is now rapidly created, shared, developed, accessed and collaborated on through and by the power of human networks (contacts). It is a two-way, fluid (editable), active, 'now' exchange." [2]

If we put all of this together we can begin to appreciate the power of adding social networking and other associated technologies to an enterprise, at least for a certain number of roles, and not just managerial knowledge workers, but those whose jobs contain significant numbers of variables. As many of these roles are more frontline rather than managerial positions which are to some extent more removed from the churn of activities, you can see where and how instant messaging, Twitter and social networks are creeping into the enterprise.

Maybe it's time to stop assuming from a more managerial standpoint that these are just distracting "toys." Maybe it's time to do some serious investigation into how social networking can be used beneficially in business. The barrier? It's the fear of managers finding that they are not "in the know" and that their staffs know more about circumstances than they do.

Overcome the barriers what might you find? Think of the potential power of each individual as if they're acting as a real-time "sensor" of circumstances. If this can be harnessed throughout the enterprise and blended with knowledge management systems, the opportunity to enhance the quality of decision making grows exponentially. It's not quite "crowd sourcing" because it should be a careful selection of a sub-section of the crowd who is relevant and contextual to the situation. Now, by most definitions of "being in the know," that is "intelligence."

As a footnote, just consider that in most enterprises we hear the tale that smokers are the best informed group. Why? Because they form a social network across the enterprise that meets regularly outside the building in their little external circles to exchange information. In fact one nonsmoking engineer at a high-tech company in Connecticut used to hang out at the outdoor smoking area just for that reason. Now, even the nonsmokers can hang out in the Cloud to keep in the know.

It's a Matter of Trust

"And that's the way it is, Friday, March 6, 1981."
—Walter Cronkite, final newscast of his 19-year *CBS Evening News.*

As a lone voice on issues such as Vietnam and Watergate, Walter Cronkite caught a lot of flack by speaking the truth on these issues in spite of the fact that industry and the Fourth Estate (the press) had become too cozy. By rising above corporate and political interests and speaking the truth, Cronkite changed the course of history and became known as the "most trusted" man in America.

Too often, it seems "trust" is no longer the way it is. Think Iraq war and weapons of mass destruction. Think the banking and financial services industry bailouts of 2008. The human condition, on the other hand, is and must be based on trust. If we no longer trust corporations, politicians or the press, where will the human need for trust be nourished? Who is the most trusted man or woman in America in the 21st century? —You!

The online competitive intelligence service, Hitwise, showed statistics indicating that Facebook beat Google in early 2010 as the most visited Web site. Hmm? Is finding a supplier on Google with search being overtaken with recommendation for a good supplier from *You* on Facebook?

The ability to manipulate information outside the body
is a mark of mankind.
But there's more to it than just manipulating information.
Humans are intensely social creatures
that crave social interactions—just consider
the most harsh of punishments, solitary confinement.

Did you know?

- Did you know... The first commercial text message was sent in December of 1992. Today, the number of text messages sent and received *every day* exceeds the total population of the planet (6+ billion).
- Did you know... It took Radio 38 years to reach a market audience of 50 million people... It took television 13 years to reach the same... It took the Internet 4 years... The iPod 3 years... And Facebook 2 years.
- Did you know... The top 10 in-demand jobs in 2010 did not exist in 2004. We are currently preparing students for jobs that don't yet exist, with technologies that haven't been invented, in order to solve problems we don't even know are problems yet.
- Did you know... The U.S. Department of Labor estimates that today's learner will have 10-14 jobs, by the age of 38. 1 in 4 workers have been with their current employer for less than a year. 1 in 2 workers have been there less than five years.
- Did you know... One million books are published every year.
- Did you know... There are over 300 million registered users on Facebook.. If Facebook were a country, it would be the 4th largest in the world (between the U.S.A. and Indonesia)
- Did you know... The #1 ranked country in Broadband Internet Penetration is Bermuda. #19 is the United States.
- Did you know... The cost of one gigabyte (GB) of storage has been decreasing at an exponential rate from $569 in 1992 to $0.13 in 2008. "Since 1982, the price of storage has dropped by a factor of 3.6 million ... to put that in context, if gas prices fell by the same amount, today, a gallon of gas would take you around the earth 2,200 times." [3]
- Did you know... One out of eight married couples met online in 2008.
- Did you know... in 2006 there were 2.8 billion Google searches each month. Now there are 31 billion. Who did we ask B.G. (Before Google?)
- Did you know... in the last 5 minutes 694 thousand songs were downloaded from the Internet – illegally!
- Did you know...while traditional newspaper circulation has

dropped by 7 million over the last two decades, online advertising has reached over 30 million readers.

- Did you know... It's easier than ever to reach a large audience, but harder than ever to really "connect" with it.[4]

> And that's the way it is,
> Friday the Thirteenth, November, 2009.
> What does all this mean?

Social Constructionism and Collectivism

Social constructionism focuses on the "truths" that are "created" through the interactions of a group. Social constructs are the by-products of countless human interactions and choices rather than laws resulting from nature, as revealed in science. Social constructionism is about the categorical structure of reality—the ways individuals and groups participate in the creation of their *perceived* reality that ultimately becomes institutionalized and made into tradition. Socially constructed reality is an ongoing, dynamic process. Reality is reproduced by people acting on their interpretations. In short, people are driven by stories and those narratives lead to social constructionism.

In their book, *Animal Spirits*, Nobel laureate George Akerlof and Yale economist Robert Shiller write, "Our sense of reality, of who we are and what we are doing, is intertwined with the story of our lives and of the lives of others. The aggregate of such stories is a national or international story, which itself plays an important role in the economy."[5] In 2001, Akelof, a professor at the University of California, Berkeley, shared the Nobel Prize with Michael Spence and Joseph Stiglitz for his work on "asymmetric information," which means that some parties to a transaction know more about the deal than others. An example is the used-car salesman who knows more about the shortcomings of the vehicle he is trying to sell than the customer he is pitching. Lemon laws grew out of such findings to protect consumers. Today consumers are protecting themselves by using the Social Web—the days of asymmetric information favoring the seller are over.

As a business that wants to adapt to the way it now is, it cannot seek a fool's paradise of the past where society's information was dispensed top-down through centralized control via the press and advertising. As Kermit Pattison reported in the *New York Times*, "Your customers are talking about you — and the whole world is listening. 'Social media for business now is life or death,' said Dan Simons, a restaurateur in the Washington area who closely monitors these forums. 'You could open a business and do everything right, but if you're unaware of these social media you will perish. Social media can take a business and put a bullet in it. Customers are abuzz with opinions — the only question is whether that buzzing reaches your ears. The first step is to tune in.'" [6]

> If you are a brand-name company and
> have a gorgeous and sophisticated Web site,
> your company's Web site is the *last place* customers go
> to get informed and make purchasing decisions.

In his personal blog, Forrester Research analyst, Jeremiah, Owyang posted an eye-opening entry, "How To Evolve Your Irrelevant Corporate Website." See Appendix B for the blog entry. [7]

Social Software, the Social Web, Social Networking, Social Media or whatever you want to call it is all about communities of shared interest, collaboration, and community member generated content. This is the "participatory society," the democratization of the press.

It's in these communities where business reputations are determined by customer ratings and opinions. It's in these digital communities where bloggers become "the press." Members of these communities aren't just outside your company, your employees join in the fray whether your management knows it or not.

Why should you bother if you've already decided not to tiptoe into the Cloud? Although you may not know it, people in your business units are already working in the Cloud. It just takes, at the most a credit card, at the least it's free, and in an instant, you can form groups, wikis, blogs and other social media—Ning.com, anyone? (Ning.com is an online platform for people to create their own social networks). No IT department approval needed, no six-month feasibility studies. Don't think it can happen? Then reflect what launched salesforce.com on the road to success. Sales people made their own decisions on where value lay and put down their own money to improve their own performances.

But, oops, no corporate governance. Back in the 1940s, computing pioneer Grace Hooper stated the justification, "It's easier to ask forgiveness than it is to get permission." [8]

Wikipedia, Flickr, and Twitter aren't just revolutions in online social media. They're the vanguard of a cultural movement as described by the founding editor of Wired magazine, Kevin Kelly. In his article, *The New Socialism: Global Collectivist Society Is Coming Online*, Kelly pushes off of media theorist Clay Shirky's hierarchy of new social arrangements. 1) Sharing 2) Cooperation 3) Collaboration and 4) Collectivism. Kelly concludes, "Rather than viewing technological socialism as one side of a zero-sum trade-off between free-market individualism and centralized authority, it can be seen as a cultural OS [operating system] that elevates both the individual and the group at once. The largely unarticulated but intuitively understood goal of communitarian technology is this: to maximize both individual autonomy and the power of people working together. Thus, digital socialism can be viewed as a third way that renders irrelevant the old debates.

"For the first time in years, the s-word is being uttered by TV pundits and in national news magazines as a force in U.S. politics. Obviously, the trend toward nationalizing hunks of industry, instituting national health care, and jump-starting job creation with tax money isn't wholly due to techno-socialism. But the last election demonstrated the power of a decentralized, webified base with digital collaboration at its core." See Appendix C for a summary of Kelly's thought-provoking article.

Kelly's vision of digital socialism won't happen overnight, but it does make it clear that enterprises should begin engaging in two-way conversations now if they want to evolve along with the global society. Small steps are in order.

JetBlue offers conversations providing travel tips and discounts on Twitter. Dell offers exclusive discounts both through

Twitter and Facebook. Whole Foods provides recipes. All these examples utilize social networking. As Ian Sherr reported on Reuters, "What's challenging, however, is that there is not one simple answer for any of these companies. Each seems to have taken some of these basic principles and applied them to their own brand to create interestingly different outcomes. But each of the successful ones has the same strategy in the end: *conversation*. Most of the top brands on Facebook all create original content, post comments, or respond to customers through social networking to increase the conversation about their company and products." [9] It's now time to start talking *with* your customers, not just talking *at* them.

According to Internet marketing veteran Paul Cheney there are only two metrics that count in your social media experimentation, "Are you causing a conversation? Are Sales going up? All others are fluff." [10]

Cheney sites the following statistics: "A recent SmartBrief on Social Media poll asked the question: What is the most important metric to track in social media? The results found that 'virality' and 'sentiment' predominated, not ROI:

- Virality (the reach of your brand and how much your message is spread), 35%
- Sentiment (positive, negative or indifferent consumer reaction), 32%
- Financials (the effect social media has on your bottom line), 20%
- Volume (number of comments, blog posts, tweets, links, etc. about your brand), 11%
- Other, 2%

"There's a lot of talk these days about measuring social media. I've even suggested that the 'warm and fuzzy, touchy-feely' days of social media are over. The CEO wants to know the ROI! Having said that, I still believe there are some things that aren't subject to statistical scrutiny."

Cheney continues, "One of my favorite songs from years past, *Matters of the Heart*, comes from singer, songwriter Bob Bennett.

The chorus goes, 'You can show me your sales curve, plot my life on a flowchart, but there's just some things that numbers can't measure, matters of the heart. We marketers put a lot of emphasis on sales curves (ROI) and such things as behavioral targeting (i.e., plotting someone's life on a flowchart as it were). But, there is a quality about social media that is very hard to define. It's a 'secret sauce' that makes it very special. For lack of a better term, I refer to it as a 'matter of the heart.'"

In her book, *Share This! How You Will Change the World with Social Networking,* media technologist Deanna Zandt takes on the issue of ROI for Social Networks and Social Media. (See Appendix D).

But wait.

There's more to Social Networks than two-way conversations.

Social Networks as a Place Where Work Gets Done

It's in the new digital communities in the Cloud where product innovation is customer driven and value is "co-produced." As Forrester Research analyst, Jeremiah Owyang explains, "Companies of the Future will collaboratively design products with customers using Web tools. These products will meet the specific needs of the people, reduce costs, and streamline the go-to-market process." One online manifestation of this is called Dell IdeaStorm, which nods to Sun Microsystems' Johnathan Schwartz's mantra that "intranets are anachronisms." The Web is a platform that can allow customers and companies to build products efficiently and quickly using real time feedback.

Think *"prosumer" (producer–consumer)* and the co-production of value. The role of producers and consumers begin to blur and merge. In a July, 2009 *BusinessWeek* article, Innovation Editor Reena Jena explained, "It's hard to get tangible results from social media. Giants from Coca-Cola to Wal-Mart Stores have set up Web sites where customers can share their interest in the brand. But many of these sites don't attract enough visitors to form a real community or have been slammed by critics, as was the case at schoolyourway.walmart.com. The retailer killed it in 2006 after just three months.

"Unlike many other companies, however, Intuit seems to have figured out a way to benefit from social media. Its insight: Rather than inviting the whole world, the accounting software maker funnels only diehard users of QuickBooks to a site where they can exchange truly helpful information. For customers, that means quicker answers to problems. For the company, this volunteer army means less need for paid technicians. 'What Intuit is doing is cutting-edge,' says Mikolaj J. Piskorski, a strategy professor at Harvard Business School.

"Intuit's QuickBooks Live Community is accessible automatically to anyone who opens QuickBooks 2009 on a PC or Mac. The site is similar to macrumors.com or macfixit.com – independent forums where Apple fans can trade tips – except that it's owned and monitored by the company.

"Intuit chose this 'narrowcast' approach after Chief Executive Brad Smith heard what was going on at the Web site of Intuit's popular TurboTax product. Customers were not only asking technical questions, they were often outshining Intuit's own tech support staff by answering 40% of the queries themselves.

"Since the latest edition of QuickBooks went on sale last October, traffic on its channel has tripled. At any time, 70% of customer service questions are answered by other QuickBooks owners, says Scott K. Wilder, who oversees the social network. Michelle L. Long of Lee's Summit, Missouri, is often on the site. The 45-year-old accountant has posted more than 5,600 answers.

"The social aspect of the program seems to have helped sales. The Mountain View (Calif.) company has sold 1 million units of QuickBooks at $200 apiece, boosting the software's market share by 4 points, to 94%. All that free tech support is saving Intuit money as well. Wilder points out that since Intuit's community outreach began, 'the number of calls to our customer service lines has been reduced. We don't give out numbers, but there have been cost savings.'"[11]

In response to Jena's article, one reader, Paul, added a valuable insight, "Ingenious in the sense that the only people that can contribute are those that really have had actual exposure to and used the product first hand. By inviting the public to a truly open forum where the advice may or may not apply, a company can hurt its reputation or that of its product if a customer continuously subjects themselves to incorrect or inconsistent tips and advice."

Mob-rule constructionism must be managed, especially considering that sockpuppets of your competitors will be ready to pounce. (A sockpuppet is a false online identity used for purposes of deception within an online community. Through the false identity a community member speaks while pretending to be a different person, like a ventriloquist manipulating a hand puppet).

> The Social Web can be more than a place where two-way dialogs happen. Moreover, it can also be the place where work gets done. Your *cloudsourced* customers become your service representatives, your call-center in the sky with world-class experts at little or no cost.

Social Networks as a Place
Where Innovation Gets Done

Many people attribute great creative achievement to *genius*, whatever that really means. Genius is often perceived as the thinking that goes on inside the heads of people like Edison and Newton, or in modern times the likes of Apple's Steve Jobs. Unfortunately, mainstream psychology hasn't been able to throw much light on what genius actually is. However a new paradigm is emerging that directly challenges a major assumption of most current theories of creative thinking, namely that the intelligence that drives it is located exclusively inside the head (the Mind-Inside-the-Head [MITH] model).

Leading philosophers and mind/brain scientists like Daniel Dennett and Andy Clark argue that contrary to both the academic and commonsense view, the mind extends out into the world. As Clark succinctly puts it, "We use intelligence to structure our environment so we can succeed with less intelligence. Our brains make the world smart so we ourselves can be dumb in peace." Once we recognize the existence of external sources of intelligence, we can begin to conceive of creative thinking in a radically new way. Put briefly, creative breakthroughs typically occur when we successfully transfer part of the intelligence embedded in our smart world from one domain to another. What Clark means is that we rely on all kinds of tools (slide rules), cultural artifacts (the Arabic number system), easy to use knowledge-embedded objects (maps) and so forth, to help lighten the computational load on our minds. Which brings us to the subject of hotspots in the networked idea-spaces of the extended mind and the "strength of weak ties."

"The strength of weak ties" is the term coined in 1973 by Mark Granovetter in what many now regard as a seminal work defining "social" collaboration. Strong ties represent the people you are closest to – coworkers, nuclear family, friends and so on. Weak ties are connections to people that you may occasionally come across – a friend's friend or online communities that share special interests outside of your ordinary interests. Granovetter argues that strong social ties are good for exerting power, but because they contain a lot of redundant information they are almost useless for gaining fresh information, new perspectives and insights – the raw materials for innovation. In contrast, weak ties contain much less redundant information and are often more important for gaining fresh information, connecting new dots and thinking outside your own box.

The interactions with previous IT collaboration tools have focused on "strong ties," building the capabilities for relationships between known people around known topics in a manner that provides a structure to deliver value. This remains an important aspect of workflow, but if we consider the emerging Social Networks, then it becomes clear that something different, something unstructured, something unknown is needed to bring new value to the table.

As reported by Patty Azzarello, a former general manager at HP, "A large network of 'weak connections' is more valuable than a small network of close connections. And it is not just a matter of the numbers. The people you are close to are not always very useful to help you because they tend to be in the same environments, know the same people, and think similarly to you. Whereas your 'weak connections' have access to different stuff, people, places and things."

Okay, having read this dialog so far, you are now determined to set up a company blog and wiki so your customers can do your customer support work for you. And now that you have dispensed with the MITH myth, you'll open a Facebook account, get LinkedIn, create your avatar in Second Life and start Tweeting so you can tap the flow of *information spaces* far and wide to do your innovation thinking for you.

Yea, right!

Your boss just might be right about a lot of this Social Networking stuff – it's nonsense.

Besides, in tough economic times we've got real work to do just to keep our heads above water. So, okay, tell your boss you agree he or she is right that this social networking stuff is indeed nonsense.

But beware – two rights can make a wrong.

It's wrong to think the dramatic and unexpected changes we are experiencing in today's world will somehow fade away and we'll return to business as usual. There's no going back to the good ole days. Innovate or fade away. It's time to tap the power of weak ties as a catalyst for innovation.

But wait! Where's the "operating manual" for Social Networking? Well, there isn't one just yet – no best practices. But new works are beginning to appear. For example, Richard Ogle's *Smart World: Breakthrough Creativity and the New Science of Ideas* provides several "laws" for coming to grips with Social Networks. Although *Smart World* tends to be a theory-based, academic look at the subject, it contains some fairly deep insights and proffers Ogle's laws for Social Networks. Check out excerpts at: tinyurl.com/yjjb4zm

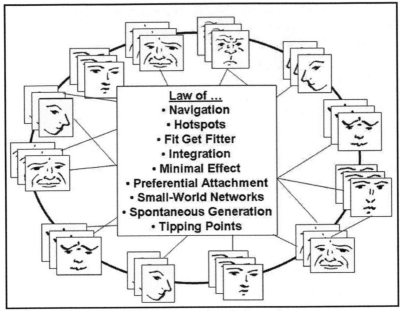

Ogle's Laws for Social Networks

One final caveat, *crowdsourcing* doesn't in any way replace the individual in the process of innovation. The idea that a mob is smarter than an individual or a focused team does not compute. Crowdsourcing is perhaps better named as *crowdsearching* for it's not the crowd that proposes innovative ideas; it's individuals found in the crowd, especially those discovered through weak ties as we discussed above.

To Twitter or Not to Twitter

In 2009, Gartner, generally considered one of the most conservative of the IT industry analysts, published a report offering some best practice guidelines for the use of "Twitter" in enterprises. This was in response to the growing number of client requests seeking advice on the topic due to the rising use of the Twitter micro blogging service among company employees. In its report, Gartner stated that up to 80% of social computing platforms will (a) incorporate micro blogging and (b) that it will be a normal part of business operations.

Many senior executives may ask why are so many employees using social computing tools in their enterprise given that they have email and such? After all, senior managers are driving business through the use of proven procedural tools. Work is sent to their employees in formats that they understand, the number of their direct reports is finite, and the place of work is usually static and desk-based. Above all, the effort to learn about a situation is normally delegated and the results delivered to managers in a manner that they have requested and understand. In this situation, there is little direct value in ad hoc collaboration that Social Networking tools provide.

By contrast, managers and workers lower in the organization often do not work at the same desk while dealing with a mixture of events and issues that do not fit into existing organizational procedures. Indeed, it is their job to figure out how, where and with whom they should work to find the right fit for the procedures. Furthermore, all of this happens in a dynamic environment.

The Web 1.0 model of storing, searching, and using content helps to an extent. However, what is really required is the Web 2.0 model of finding people with knowledge and expertise before identifying the relevant content. E-mail has been and continues to be used for this purpose. However, too many emails can clog the system, too many are irrelevant to an individual's work and far too much time is wasted.

Web 1.0 showed how search engines could be used to find the required content. Then, RSS feeds were used to deliver the selected content as and when it was updated. On the other hand, Social Networks "store" the characteristics of people and their interests and knowledge so that individuals can find the right person or group of people relevant to a given issue. Micro blogging, which is what Twitter provides, can be seen as the equivalent of a RSS feed.

In short, the faster and more frequent the activities and business challenges, the less formal procedures are able to supply the first stage of answers. Furthermore, it is less likely that content or case studies will be perfectly captured for reuse and, typically, a response from the right person with the right experience and expertise needed to provide guidance will be slow.

Therefore the reason staff and operational managers adopt social networking becomes clearer. However, at the same time, the inability to understand the exact issues being addressed and the manner of resolving these issues using an unknown medium and method remains a barrier for senior managers. Senior managers may find that a more formal approach to adopting social computing by setting out definable business goals may be more acceptable and understandable. Indeed, they are right to be wary of the possibility of unforeseen consequences and damage to the enterprise resulting from an ad hoc uptake of Social Computing.

The following charter was set up by a group of companies led by Intel and has been made publicly available as a generic adoption model to help enterprises take a well-managed adoption path in a manner that can be understood to create value around specified enterprise business goals.

1. *Employees want to put a face to a name:* Intel is a large, globally dispersed workforce of approximately 85,000 employees. Global teams of people work together but in many cases would not recognize a team member if they passed them on the street.

2. *Too much time is lost trying to find people and information to do your job:* The average Intel employee loses one day a week trying to find people with the experience and expertise, plus the relevant information, to do his or her job. We have calculated some of the monetary impact due to lost productivity and opportunity. Let's just say that it is motivating us to take action.

3. *Getting work done effectively in globally dispersed teams is challenging:* There is usually a window of two hours a day that team members can communicate in real time with each other. Work-in-progress collaboration is often done via email, passing back and forth edited presentation decks, and crossing discussion wires. Task hand-offs from one team leaving work and another entering are very rough.

4. *New hires want to have a way to integrate into Intel faster:* This is not a generational thing. Think back to your first day at your company. How did you learn about the company? How did you put a name to a face or discover who you needed to connect with?

Did you feel isolated and lost? I bet you answered yes to most or all of these questions. It is a fact that if you improve the integration experience, you will get faster engagement, happier employees, and quicker delivery of solid results.

5. *Restructuring and employee redeployment impacts organizational health:* The last two years, Intel has spent restructuring and reducing its workforce. With the current economic conditions, now all companies are faced with and are embarking upon the same venture. This leaves employees feeling disconnected, isolated, and disengaged. We are finding value in providing opportunities for Intel to feel small, give employees a voice, and build a sense of community.

6. *We reinvent the wheel over and over again:* Need we say more? Stovepipes and silos breed redundancy.

7. *We learn more via on the job training than we do in a classroom:* Providing employees with the opportunities to share their knowledge and their expertise allows other employees to organically discover information to help them do their jobs. Your organization becomes a learning organization with "wisdom of the crowds" at its core.

8. *We need to deliver radical innovation in a mature company:* It is challenging for mature companies like Intel to find a parallel innovation vein to the current incremental innovation. However, it is essential in order to power future growth. In Judy Estrin's book, *Closing the Innovation Gap: Reigniting the Spark of Creativity in a Global Economy*, she states the five core values of innovation are questioning, risk-taking, openness, patience, and trust. Intel has these values at our core but organizational stovepipes get in the way of ideas. Social tools can unleash those ideas.

9. *When the mature workforce starts to retire, they carry knowledge out the door:* Have you thought about the bottom line impact that the large amount of retiring baby boomers will have on your company? Or better yet, our economic future? Tacit knowledge is imperative to transfer knowledge. To date, there are no solid tools to effectively extract the tacit knowledge. Social tools show real promise.

The issue of exactly what Social Networking tools should be adopted will become clearer as companies experiment and gain experience. The choice that both business schools and industry technology analysts tend to focus on is whether to adopt social computing or not. Instead, they should focus on the question of how to manage the adoption for maximized strategic benefit.

How Big and How Powerful is the Social Web?

Who has the largest population on earth? We all know that the largest nation state is China with its 1.3 billion population. But the largest group tied together with a common bond is the "Internet nation," the *Internation*, with a population of almost 1.6 billion as of March 31, 2009. And, by the way, e-commerce spending was $2.8 trillion in 2008, 15% of the world's GDP. By 2012, the numbers of the *Mobile* Social Web (cell phones, smart phones et al) are forecast to grow to 975 million. [12]

In the Internation *truth* and *trust* are peer-to-peer versus higher authority, and they transcend national and corporate boundaries. Social constructionism supersedes authority.

Just consider the news. The explosive growth of social networking has fundamentally changed our relationship with news—now *we* are the press. News is no longer something we passively take in. We now engage with news, react to news, and share news—even create the news. News has become an important element of community. It's something around which we gather, connect, and converse. Now we can all become part of the evolution of a news story, expanding it with comments and links to relevant information, adding facts and differing points of view.

Reflecting on what the social networking trend means to business, we can look back to Henry Ford, the notion of mass production, and the use of mass media to push mass consumption. Today Inbound Marketing ("demand pull") is replacing Outbound Marketing (the old "supply push" marketing method). With Inbound Marketing, instead of your company finding customers, customers find your company.

Advertising, trade shows, public relations and the like give way to Twitter, Facebook, blogs and other social media. Marketing moves from the newsstand to the Cloud, and CEOs must take note. Want proof? How about this headline: "*BusinessWeek* Sale May Fetch Only $1." Reflecting the advertisers that *BusinessWeek* covers, automotive financial services, and retailing the venerable 80-year old magazine was reported up for sale, and a banker put the price tag for the sale at $1. *And that's the way it is, Monday, July 13, 2009.* [13]

The Chicago *Tribune*, the Chicago *Sun-Times*, the Philadelphia *Daily News*, the Minneapolis *Star Tribune* all recently filed for bankruptcy, while the *Miami Herald* went up for sale in December 2008. The *Boston Globe* is said to be losing $1 million a week, while the *San Francisco Chronicle* lost as much as $70 million in 2008. Hmmm, more to follow? The New York *Daily News*, the Fort Worth *Star-Telegram*, the Cleveland Plain Dealer, and the Detroit *News* round out a quick list of traditional newspapers that seem to be telling a story of mountains of debt and falling ad revenue. Where did the readers go? Where did the advertising dollars go?

The Social Web is also influencing the spending of advertising dollars in broadcast media. As a result of a swarm of petitioners triggered by the Huffington Post, the auto insurance company GEICO pulled its ads from the controversial Glenn Beck show, as did Lawyers.com, Progressive Insurance, Procter & Gamble, and SC Johnson (…update, add Wal-Mart, Best Buy, CVS, Travelocity, Allergan, Re-Bath, Bradview Security, and GMAC to the list).[14]

And it's not just the media being affected by demand pull versus supply push marketing. How about the new car lot? Potential customers take considerable time visiting multiple car lots when they are in the market for a new automobile. And the haggling begins. Used cars have long been sold via the Net, but in August 2009, a troubled dinosaur of the auto industry, began a new way of letting customers haggle over *new* cars. GM formed a partnership with eBay, gm.ebay.com. As reported in Reuters, "The website allows consumers to compare pricing across models and participating dealerships, negotiate prices, and arrange financing and payment. Consumers can agree to pay the advertised price or indicate the price they are willing to pay and can negotiate online with the dealer for the vehicle. More than 20,000 new Chevrolet, Buick,

GMC and Pontiac vehicles will be listed initially on the site." [15] Let the haggling begin—in the Cloud instead of the car lot.

But there's even more than humans involved in what's emerging as a massive-scale Web-based computing platform. The Internet is also becoming the Internet of *things*. In addition to the explosive rise of Web-capable smart cell phones, e-books and net books, billions of sensors, RFID tags and other digital technologies are being embedded into all sorts of things in the *physical world*. Smart cars, smart appliances, smart cameras, smart highways, smart manufacturing equipment. RFID tagged goods tracked throughout the supply chain. Where's my runaway Fido?

With billions of people and probably soon trillions of things connected to the Web, the physical world will converge with the digital world and the Cloud as a platform will become more like Yale professor David Gelernter's 1992 classic book, *Mirror Worlds: or the Day Software Puts the Universe in a Shoebox*. The implications of digital technologies penetrating every physical and ethereal aspect of the economy and society are enormous.

Putting It All Together

Let's repeat some comments from the opening of this chapter, "Before we can properly discuss the changing role of information technology in business, we need to set the context of what's happening in the larger world *outside* business, what's happening in our hyper-connected society as a result of dramatic advances brought about by the Internet."

As Aronica and Ramdoo exclaim in their book, *The World is Flat?* (www.mkpress.com/flat), "Globalization is the greatest reorganization of the world since the Industrial Revolution." Globalization is far more than multinational corporations going to the ends of the earth in search of cheap labor. Jeremy Rifkin likens the emerging trend in globalization to the *Third Industrial Revolution*, and it starts with society itself. So here are some snippets from Rifkin, and *keep in mind that as society goes, so goes business and commerce*. "The pivotal turning points in human consciousness occur when new energy regimes converge with new communications revolutions, creating new economic eras.

"The new communications revolutions become the command and control mechanisms for structuring, organizing, and managing more complex civilizations that the new energy regimes make possible. For example, in the early modern age, print communication became the means to organize and manage the technologies, organizations, and infrastructure of the coal, steam and rail revolution. It would have been impossible to administer the first industrial revolution using script and codex.

"Communication revolutions not only manage new, more complex energy regimes, but also change human consciousness in the process. Forager/hunter societies relied on oral communications, and their consciousness was mythologically constructed. The great hydraulic agricultural civilizations were, for the most part, organized around script communication and steeped in theological consciousness. The first industrial revolution of the 19th century was managed by print communication, and ushered in ideological consciousness. Electronic communication became the command and control mechanism for arranging the second industrial revolution in the 20th century and spawned psychological consciousness.

"Today, we are on the cusp of another historic convergence of energy and communication – a third industrial revolution – that could extend empathic sensibility to the biosphere itself and to all of life on Earth. The distributed Internet revolution is coming together with distributed renewable energies, making possible a sustainable, post-carbon economy that is both globally connected and locally managed.

"Schoolchildren everywhere are learning that their everyday behavior – the food they eat, the electricity they use, the family car they ride in, and myriad other consumer habits – intimately affect the wellbeing of every other human being and every other creature on Earth. This is the emergence of biosphere consciousness and the beginning of the next stage of our evolutionary journey."

Read more here: http://tinyurl.com/y8epkld
and here: http://tinyurl.com/yew9cjv

When the Industrial Revolution took hold in the U.S.A., farmers railed against the railroads for building steel highways through their pastures, disrupting the natural rhythms of their cattle. Now that we are entering Rifkin's Third Industrial Age, Social Networks are disrupting the natural rhythms of our current hydrocarbon supply-push economy. We have crossed the threshold to an uncertain future, and those that will tune into the 37 signals* in the Human Network just may find the future of intelligent business.

---

* Search for Extra-Terrestrial Intelligence (SETI) is the collective name for a number of activities people undertake to search for extraterrestrial life. Mankind constantly analyzes radio waves from outer space in the search for extraterrestrial intelligence. Since this analysis started, almost all of the signal sources have been identified. 37 signals, however, remain unexplained.

Takeaway

As we fuse the physical world with the digital world in the Cloud, and recognize that the Human Network means that *You* are the Web, trust becomes the high-octane fuel for economic activity. As we've explored, trust emerges from social constructionism forged by our communities.

We turn to Frits Bussemaker, Chairman of the BPM-Forum Netherlands and Kostmos to summarize some actionable points, "On the supplier side of the business, a company can have "trust" documented in a service-level agreement (SLA) but, that only works if you have a specific transaction. On the other hand, if you go for co-creation, joint development and dialog, the SLA actually works against you! So, you need to cope with the trust and really, really share all the information needed.

"The 'currency' of community is *time* and not money. Companies need to invest time to gain value out of their communities. Time? In the past, corporate communication was one-way, from one-to-many in the form of advertising, PR, and so on. Today, companies must establish two-way, ongoing dialogs with their customers, suppliers, trading partners, and other stakeholders. Such community dialogs require an investment in time, in direct participation in new social networks, wikis, and blogs. And not just time from a public relations department, but also from the leadership and the experts of the company.

"By having open and meaningful dialogs with the members of their communities, companies can build trust. Trust is something money cannot buy. It takes an investment in time, not money, to build and nurture communities. Communities, and the connections formed in communities, must have a purpose and provide mutual value to all community members. A new management approach is needed to create and manage communities, where all organizations that evolve from 'Corporations' to 'Cooperations' will profit and find their time well spent. [16]

Trust is the cornerstone of today's global economy, *and that's the way it is—in the 21st century.*

References.

[1] http://www.cisco.com/web/about/humannetwork/index.html

[2] http://www.freepint.com/bookshelf/know.htm

[3] www.zdnetasia.com/insight/specialreports/smb/storage/0,3800011754,620 34356,00.htm

[4] http://www.youtube.com/watch?v=cL9Wu2kWwSY

[5] http://press.princeton.edu/chapters/i8967.html

[6] http://www.nytimes.com/2009/07/30/business/smallbusiness/30reputatio n.html?_r=1&hpw

[7] http://www.web-strategist.com/blog/2007/05/29/web-strategy-how-to-evolve-your-irrelevant-corporate-website/

[8] http://twitter.ulitzer.com/node/1049930

[9] http://blogs.reuters.com/shop-talk/2009/08/04/social-media-for-business/

[10] http://www.socialmediatoday.com/SMC/121162

[11] http://www.businessweek.com/magazine/content/09_28/b41390663653 00.htm

[12] http://www.internetworldstats.com/stats.htm

[13] http://www.ft.com/cms/s/0/bd68cdc6-6fdc-11de-b835-00144feabdc0.html

[14] http://www.huffingtonpost.com/james-rucker/geico-pulls-its-ads-from_b_256724.html

[15] http://www.reuters.com/article/newsOne/idUSTRE5792N920090810

[16] http://tinyurl.com/ocbf4r

4. From Information Technology to Business Technology

The next IT platform shift and a really big question:
"Why is Consumer IT so simple and Enterprise IT so complex?"

Key Points: From Transactions to Interactions

Software that supports both end user and developer tasks becomes more intuitive and responsive to change. Cloud computing blends together the power of the Web 2.0 and service-oriented development by distributing Web services across the Internet and allowing the services to interoperate as a unified whole. This advanced infrastructure can empower businesses to construct new-era applications that were once technically impractical. Simply stated, many collaborative and other new-era business applications would not be feasible without a cloud computing infrastructure. These applications are highly collaborative and integrate (mashup) resources from many systems, often outside the enterprise.

Further, service-oriented computing in the Cloud can integrate multiple problem-solving paradigms, such as logic-based, procedural and constraint satisfaction. But organizations should not be misled. Cloud computing is as much a way of thinking as it is a service-oriented infrastructure. Without a corresponding paradigm shift, a change in thinking, the associated tools and techniques will not generate the desired results.

But there is an even bigger point to grasp, and that is how the nature of work itself is changing. Having successfully automated the back office processes the focus is now on empowering the knowledge workers in the front office. Collaboration is now the key to competitive advantage and the Cloud is where collaboration takes place.

A Mesh of Connections

Today, thanks to the Internet, it's possible to visualize the business and indeed the consumer world as a Mesh of connections among people as well as content, enterprises and procedures. Collaboration across this Mesh is unstructured and for navigation relies on the principles of Social Networks in which people characterize themselves in various ways. The more that people are enrolled in Social Networks with their interests, expertise and experiences profiled, then the better the opportunity to find an optimal connection. It is at this point that a reversal of the usual business principle of structured, closed, and well-focused groups starts to apply. Limit the people and you will limit the experiences that can be tapped. To many business managers this deliberate defocusing seems entirely contrary to their training and experience.

Looking back, the introduction of the networked PC heralded the start of Matrix Management, the ability for a person to perform his or her particular activity not only within the confines of a single department, but across the enterprise. This flexibility was coupled with redesigning business models to optimize processes horizontally across the enterprise, instead of being broken up to departmental silos. Email was used as a key tool in the support of Matrix work and many early email directories listed not just people by name, but by role as well. The stability of the external business environment allowed for the optimization of internal working practices in alignment with internal business processes.

Looking forward, the highly dynamic, unstable external markets of today have drastically shifted the emphasis to the ability to adapt to events and circumstances quickly, and to reorient to the next situation as it arises. The relative stability of a person with a specific role is still working in some areas of the enterprise, but clearly not in other areas. In broad terms using IT to automate and administer back office transactions with accuracy at the lowest cost continues to work effectively because stability is a key attribute. Those charged with running these areas are faced with strict audit and compliance standards, to say nothing of legal requirements relating to certain data. With the rise of social computing, IT staffs may feel the need to "protect" the enterprise from this new wave of technology as it seems to undermine their very important roles.

On the other hand, those facing the external world from front office areas such as sales, marketing, supply chain management and so on, now find themselves confronted with an ever-changing set of events that they must master. Their success depends on not just understanding what is going on, but actually being able to optimize circumstances to create winning positions. The speed of change means that it is almost impossible to redesign and recreate enterprise rules and procedures fast enough to keep up. The challenge is that the external markets and events are unstructured, as are the people who are involved in them. That is not to say that the individuals are themselves without specific responsibilities, but there is no formal organization chart across connected enterprises trading together (virtual enterprise networks). Add in the increasing number of direct consumer channels where customers want products and services "their way," and the idea of being able to build and operate structured processes with people in specific roles within these processes is obviously flawed.

The goal is to enable people to make the expertise and responsibilities of front office workers known to other people. This idea is not new. In fact it's the very basis for traditional commodity markets. What is new is the requirement to recognize people with the appropriate expertise and responsibilities – even if they are unknown to you.

Large enterprises increasingly have to be able to leverage their internal intellectual property and expertise as the key to competitive differentiation and execution. As such they need to be able to move across their own internal barriers by creating the equivalent of internal trading markets so that their best people can be identified for any given situation. This requirement represents the next logical step in extending the ideas of Matrix Management toward Collaborative Management.

Matrix Management was driven by Business Process Reengineering, utilizing the technology revolution of the PC and enterprise networks. Collaborative Management is being driven by the adoption of Cloud-enabled business models and another technology revolution we'll call Business Technology (BT).

The Relationships Among Existing and New Technologies

We started the preceding chapter by examining the external world and collaboration technology is changing almost every aspect of life and business. This is the world in which our enterprise must now do business. This is the world from which our enterprise must employ people. This is the world in which our enterprise must find other business partners. Above all, this is the world in which our enterprise must win its share of customers and markets.

These pressures translate into internal changes, new working practices, the adoption of new technologies and new funding models. To explore these changes, let's start with the comparison of the last technology revolution, the networked PC, and what is happening now in the Cloud

Here we want to focus on the role of cloud computing in creating *value* for the enterprise. The size and scope of the external environment and ecosystem of an enterprise offers huge untouched capabilities for improvement that far outweigh the impact of further rounds of cost cutting, a course of action that is already experiencing the law of diminishing returns.

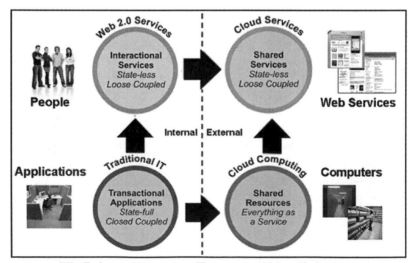

The Relationships Among Existing and New Technologies

Traditional IT. Back in the 1990s the term Information Technology (IT) was introduced to differentiate technologies such as personal computers, networks and client-server architectures and their role in the business from the existing use of "data processing" in individual departments or data centers. The role of IT was to centralize processes, restrict and manage the unchecked distribution of data to end users' PCs, and leverage enterprise resources using enterprise systems such as Enterprise Resource Planning (ERP) to reduce cost and encourage operational efficiency. Goals in the era of Business Process Reengineering (BPR) were aligned to do "more of less" in terms of restricting activities to a few key product lines or services. Traditional IT (bottom left in the diagram) can be firmly positioned as *internal* and *cost based.*

Web 2.0 Services. The advent of Web 2.0 (top left) introduced Web usage patterns around *people and communication.* From an IT perspective, Web 2.0 in the front office represents a return to the risk of decentralization and loss of control of data that came with the introduction of PCs. This was viewed with suspicion at best from an IT perspective.

Web 2.0, although it may share some common technology elements with traditional IT, generally does not use the stateful data that is so important to maintain business controls in back-office IT operations. Web 2.0 poses little to no risk to classic IT operations, but it does introduce a range of new capabilities around people and collaboration by leveraging their expertise for value to the enterprise. As distinguished from the content technologies of Web 1.0, Web 2.0 provides a business with different sets of capabilities for adjusting to quick moving business events to achieve optimized decisions and value. From this perspective Web 2.0 positioning is internal and adds value to traditional IT.

Cloud Computing. Cloud computing, as a generic name for various forms of virtualization and remote delivery of resources, is seen by IT management as a method to reduce the costs of providing current forms of IT based mostly on "applications." The path from in-house operations through the virtualization of servers, first toward an internal Cloud, and finally an external Cloud is driven by cost reduction through increased sharing of expensive resources (bottom right).

Cloud Services. Compared to IT staff, business managers see a very different Cloud (top right) as one driven by the creation of new marketplaces in which to offer new *smart business services* that can create new and profitable revenue streams. The driving force for frontline business managers adopting cloud computing is new *value generation* versus *cost savings.* The challenge is to support these marketplaces through the flexibility of Cloud *business services* as opposed to IT *applications.* When combined, the use of Web 2.0 and the cloud computing is increasingly known as Business Technology to differentiate its role in the business from the role of traditional IT.

The implication of deploying Cloud Services (top right) is an increase in the speed and tempo of the business. This, in turn, links to the need for people to work smarter (top left) in rapidly collaborating around relevant information using their expertise to make good decisions faster. It also links to the need for a cloud computing infrastructure (bottom right) to be able to provide the needed services and capabilities as quickly as possible.

IT planning and budgeting horizons stretch for a year or more ahead with budgets costs allocated in the annual overhead plan. In using Business Technology this would be impossible as the immediate reaction to the market is the key to success. Therefore, neither forward budgeting nor static resource delivery is possible. These are the key reasons for supplying, implementing and supporting Cloud services that are billed directly to the business user as monthly operating expenses (OPEX). Business needs vary as business opportunities and challenges arise, and costs vary accordingly, reflecting the benefit of elasticity in deploying as many or as few computing resources as needed.

It now becomes much clearer as to how to choose what and where to change the game with cloud computing. But before we focus in on this, there are operational and governance issues to address. We used the previous diagram to illustrate how business focus and business intelligence was moving from being solely internally focused toward external opportunities. Now look what happens if we lay the above diagram over the one below.

To be able to operate effectively in the top right external value quadrant requires the ability to support people working differently in the top left internal value quadrant. At the same time there needs to be a new way to support these operations that is flexible and chargeable on a per-use model. This diagram brings together all of the changes and the driving forces in one set of relationships as well as illustrating the changes from the internal cost-driven support model of Traditional IT.

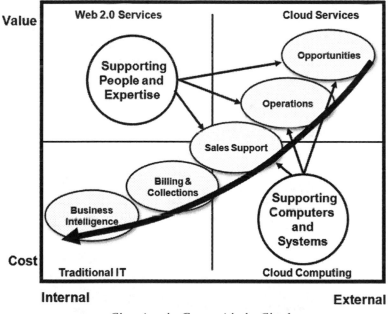

Changing the Game with the Cloud

Cloud services do in fact present a governance problem. These new external uses of Business Technology are in direct conflict with some of the core operational and organizational policies that ushered in Traditional IT and the role of the CIO in managing the distribution and use of data. Instinctively IT feels that to release control is dangerous, and in the Traditional IT application model with its strong emphasis on enterprise data and *one version of the truth,* this is entirely correct. But cloud computing is a different model built around *services* and not *applications.* Service-oriented architectures are loosely coupled, using external representations of data and not data housed in systems of records. The risks are not the same, even with the Public Cloud resourcing model. The whole environment is different and the requirement is to have the flexibility to do what is needed in the eyes of the external market.

Many business users and departments have already contracted to use externally supplied services, often without even telling their IT departments. So if the business department pays for externally provided services, then the questions of governance and management are tricky. But such questions must be asked and answered to avoid chaos and to meet audit and compliance requirements. Responsibilities for management control and auditability don't disappear into the clouds. As discussed in the next chapter, IT is well positioned to help business managers implement service-oriented techniques and methods for auditability and control of business unit usage of cloud computing.

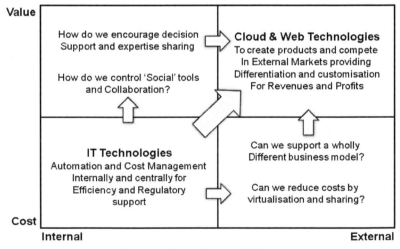

Internal Cost - External Value

Before taking a detailed look at services that lay at the heart of the new Cloud environment let's take one more look at how IT will be required to support the enterprise in key areas that include the new front-office uses of Business Technology.

2%	The Flow of New Ideas that Differentiate	**BUSINESS TECHNOLOGY**
18%	The Ability to Execute on the Ideas	**The External Market-Focused Enterprise**
80%	Capability to Operate the Resources	**INFORMATION TECHNOLOGY** Internally focused on operational exclience, cost management and compliance

Business Technology vs. Information Technology

The diagram illustrates that a traditional IT model would take a new requirement and build an entire dedicated technology stack to deliver a solution, as represented by the triangle. Now we are talking about a different approach, an approach whereby granular services are regularly and frequently re-orchestrated to support new business needs on a pay-per-use model.

A discussion on Business Technology around applying technologies to new business requirements is easily grasped by a hard-pressed business manager. Accustomed to easy-to-use Consumer IT at home, business managers are becoming accidental technologists. The leadership of an enterprise shouldn't turn a blind eye to this trend. The challenge for the enterprise is to integrate the two worlds of Consumer IT with Enterprise IT without creating chaos. To do that the expertise of IT staff is needed more than ever, but the role changes from being a back office sheriff to being a front office counselor, coach and mentor.

It's Not About Cloud *Computing*, It's About Cloud *Services*

The following is derived from an elucidating video, *The Future Internet: Service Web 3.0,* produced by STI International in Berlin.[1]

Because the current Internet is composed of unstructured sources, the Internet is broken. We still have not one Web, but a vast variety of unlinked data that is unable to communicate.

Today's "Broken" Internet

That's why the future Internet will have to change, and change it must. The new Internet will change to answer the vital question of how we share *meaning* across machines. Semantic technologies that let us distinguish the word "bank" from a river bank to a financial institution are essential.

An Internet of Meaningful "Services"

Unless semantic technologies are integrated into the Internet, we'll be overwhelmed with information glut and the Internet will not be usable.

We are also talking about the Internet of "things" like cars, sensors, goods, refrigerators and other physical objects all connected to the Internet. These "things" are linked to supply chains and business activities that lead to an improvement in business efficiency and effectiveness. The content of things (think trillions of things connected to and monitored by the Internet) and the content of people (currently 1,600,000,000 people are connected) will grow significantly and will be a driving force for the future of the Internet.

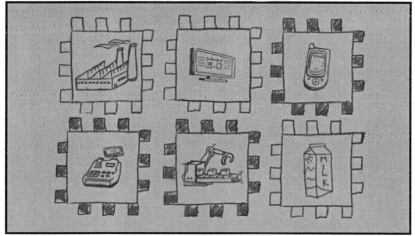

An Internet of "Things" and People

Collaborative business models and social Internet tools will make the Internet run with fewer barriers than we face today.

Intelligent semantic technologies will support these tools. Everything and everybody will be connected.

Everything, everywhere, always. We must imagine the future Internet as a service—mobile, ubiquitous and pervasive. 24/7 availability will be the norm.

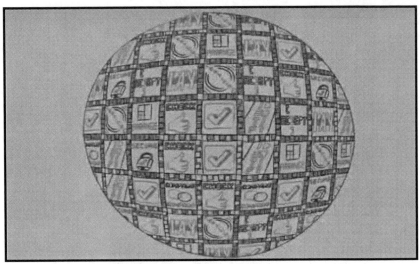

The Internet as a Service

But we need new networks that integrate all kinds of devices, bringing radical new efficiencies to economic processes. Business processes will be unified as services that can be used by different groups of people, within an enterprise or externally via the Internet of services—a mobile Internet of services and things.

The future is not about cloud *computing*, which is necessary but not sufficient—it's about *intelligent Cloud services* delivered over the Internet.

Going Mobile

The shift from the data and computer-centric world of IT to the people and communication-centric world of BT is also driving a shift in personal devices with the exploding use of smart phones and net books. Mobility isn't just about making an application available on a remote device by wireless; it's a change in life style.

If either your PC or your Smart Phone was to fail and not be available for three days which would you choose to have working? If people who were asked this question are in a *support function* they would say their PC as their work is fundamentally based at a given desk and they have access to a phone on the desk. If their roles are *operational*, they are driven by events, meeting people outside their own offices and so on, and their choice would be the Smart Phone. One observer dubbed it, "Value creating roles need to be where the event is happening; supporting roles have the process delivered to them." That observation may be little harsh, but if you examine the logic, a Smart Phone can be with you at all times. You can do email and, if you are really determined, even create documents and handle spreadsheets. But most of all you can be in touch with constantly changing circumstances and be able to direct activities. This is why it's easy to spot business people everywhere tapping away on their Smart Phones; it has become normal business behavior.

Is it now time to consider the Smart Phone as an integral part of IT? And has the IT function really mastered the integration and support that should go with this new breed of mobile devices?

The latest statistics on operating system shipments showed that the iPhone now has a market share that equates to half of the total Linux market share. That's indeed a quiet revolution and one that should encourage the IT department, with its focus on using Linux as a cost-reducing operating system to ask some questions about including the iPhone in its focus. After all, users are choosing iPhones regardless of the enterprise issues such as security. Additionally, the business tools (iPhone Apps) are appearing, such as Dataviz's popular Documents ToGo, a Microsoft Office compatible suite. To many business users the phone has become the more accessible device for them to *do their own thing* and getting *what they want the way they want it.*

Companies have done such a good job of managing the PC to stop damaging rogue activities that the users have migrated their *personalization* activities to their Smart Phones. It's no good saying that Smart Phones are not part of IT because they certainly are part of an enterprise user's activities and technology base. So an approach to enabling them to be used securely and become an integrated part of the IT environment is needed. It's time to make Smart Phones a part of IT.

Smart Phones and other wireless devices such as bar code readers should be integrated with the enterprise's IT systems. Just as IT came to include mainframes and then PCs and servers, Smart

Phones are, or should be, part of the *real estate* of Enterprise IT, or better phrased, Enterprise BT. It's amazing how many new technologies use wireless, which by integration with IT, create new business value. Notice again the business case is "value" by improving sales revenues more than "cost savings." But maybe these two can go together.

Can all of this work? Is this avalanche of technology and change in expectations and working practice really be something made to work in the favor of an enterprise to actually create more sales and value? As a reality check there is the well known example of how Wal-mart, one of the savviest retailers, has gained by supporting and enabling its front line staff to respond to in-store events and make quick decisions that boost its sales.

Wal-Mart has driven many new technologies through the hype cycle and into real value ahead of others. The Telxon, pronounced "Telzon," is a hand-held bar-code scanner with a wireless connection to the store's computer. When pointed at any product, the Telxon reveals astonishing amounts of information: the quantity that should be on the shelf, the availability from the nearest warehouse, the retail price and most amazing of all, the markup. All employees are given access to this information, because in theory at least anyone in the store can order a couple of extra pallets of anything and discount the item heavily as a Volume Producing Item (VPI), competing with other departments to rack up the most profitable sales each month. Floor clerks even have portable equipment to print their own price stickers. This is how Wal-Mart detects demand and responds to it by distributing decision-making power to the grass-roots level. It's as simple, yet as radical, as that.

One employee recounted the story of test-marketing tents that could protect cars for people who didn't have enough garage space. They sold out quickly and several customers came in asking for more. Clearly this was an exceptional case of word-of-mouth marketing, so the employee ordered a truckload of tent garages, "Which I shouldn't have done really without asking someone," he said with a shrug, "because I hadn't been working at the store for long." But the item was a huge success. His VPI was the biggest in store history – not bad for a new employee.

Now just reflect on the integration that this required. It's not just database access that's going on here. There are links to core business processes and identity management must resolve what data and processes are made available to whom. This whole integration qualifies as Business Technology. This is about significant decentralization – taking the information to as many people in as many places in the front lines of the business as needed. Front-line workers are empowered to be proactive. This is what new devices, new technologies and most of all, continuous connectivity by wireless can mean, whether it's a Blackberry in the hands of a traveling salesman or a bar-code reader in the hands of a retail clerk. Give front-line workers the right information, at the right time, in the right format, at the right place and you can drive the best possible decisions at the very spots those decisions can be most effective.

Exciting? Game changing? Necessary for business success? The answer to all these questions really ought to be yes, but is more likely a qualified yes. Why the qualification? Almost certainly because the issue of funding these moves comes at a time when IT budgets are flat or even being reduced in the midst of the greatest economic downturn since WWII.

But wait. As we've stated before, ever tightening IT budgets represent one of the strongest reasons for the shift to cloud computing and services-based delivery models. Business innovation no longer needs to be constrained by traditional IT budget models, even during tough economic times.

All this connects to another change in capabilities that is increasingly in demand: unified communications and messaging. Connecting people and their personal devices and formats means accommodating the available form factors for each and every participant, as the imposition of a single standard across not just one enterprise but across the entire globe is clearly impossible.

The ubiquitous high-bandwidth Internet connections running Internet Protocols, the increasing range of devices to make use of this capability, and the shift in focus from machine to machine networking toward people and collaboration have resulted in a complex environment. Many, if not most people today, use more than one device. These can be a combination of a work PC, a separate home PC, and a Smart Phone. Increasingly, employers are providing additional devices such as phone conferencing units and teleconferencing rooms.

Most large enterprises grow organically, usually in an unplanned manner with no serious attempt at optimizing the use of corporate bandwidth and connections. In fact, the budgets to operate all of the devices and services may well be held in different operating units with no overall view of the total costs.

Unified Communications or UC is the integration of all of the communication connections and devices into a single cohesive environment. It presents a consistent service to all devices from a cost-effective centralized resource. Even though it's technically inaccurate, comparisons have been made to this being a kind of virtualization for communication devices. However, in the context of optimizing resources, there are similarities.

Unified Messaging or UM is concerned with creating a common interface, or experience for users to hide the differences between various services running on different devices at different locations. One of the fundamental goals of UM is to ensure that any messaging service, such as voice, email, or instant messaging can be used from any device, regardless of format or location, fixed or mobile.

In practice, it is rarely possible to separate UC and UM as the two aspects are largely interdependent and most products combine them. The term "Presence" is used to indicate the ability of a UC and messaging service to understand the current location of the user in terms of the device being used and the services that can be supported.

At the Mobile World Congress 2010 in Barcelona, Google CEO Eric Schmidt explained that Google is moving forward with a "mobile first" mantra. "It's like magic. All of a sudden you can do things that it never occurred to you were possible. Our programmers are working on products from a 'Mobile First' perspective. That's a major change. Every recent product announcement we have made – and of course we have a desktop version – is being made from the point of view of it being used on a high-performance mobile phone on all the browsers that are available.

Our programmers want to work on apps for mobile that you can't get on a desktop – apps that are personal and location aware."

Look Ma, No Computer

"Miniaturization was the big theme in the First Age of computers: rising power, falling prices and computers for everybody. The theme of the Second Age is that computing transcends computers. Information travels through a sea of anonymous, interchangeable computers like a breeze through tall grass."
—Yale Professor David Gelernter, *The Second Coming*.

The automobile totally changed Western society, in good ways and bad. It changed where we worked by making commuting an everyday affair. It set us free to go where we wanted, when we wanted. The automobile transformed isolated communities to a single entity. The automobile created a mobile society and changed the very structure of the family. It also changed almost every industry from motels, to shopping malls, to supply chains, to holidays. It created the consumer society and "planned obsolescence" was born. In the 1950s, teenagers bought cars for as little as $25, which allowed them the freedom and privacy with their sweethearts to do as they pleased, leading to the loosening of the social restrictions of Victorian morals firmly in place before World War II. Today, many express who they are by the car they drive.

But for all its social impact, we don't talk about the technology under the hood, we simply grab the keys and start on our way to wherever that may be. We take the automobile for granted. The technology under the hood, the internal combustion engine and the transmission *disappear*. That's beginning to happen today with the Millennial generation and its iPods, iPhones, and net books.

When it comes to information technology on the other hand, most of us still talk about the technology: the Internet, email, PCs, wikis, and blogs. But not for long. As the Millennials become the larger segment of the population, all these technologies will "disappear" as did the internal combustion engine of the automobile. They will be taken for granted, they will become a part of us. The underlying technologies will simply disappear. We, not the computers, not the networking technologies, are the Web! We are the Human Network.

As Boston Consulting Group's George Stalk wrote, "Computers will 'understand' their users without the need for explicit, machine-language instructions. Ultimately, computers will fade into the background of human activities ... though they are constantly there, 24/7."

The result will be the democratization of media and the rise of a truly participatory society. Everyone will be a broadcaster and a publisher. Every company will be in the media business, communicating with employees, customers and suppliers. But now they had better make that communication a two-way dialog, not a one-way monolog with advertising and memoranda.

Social Companies

Social media are only tools, but on the other hand they are tools that are transforming our world. Companies must take note, they must adapt. As INHolland University professor Frans van der Reep notes, "The Internet is changing the way we organize work. It is shifting the requirement for what we call the 'schedule push' and the hierarchical organization that it implies, and therefore it is removing the type of control that is conventionally used to match resources to tasks, and customer demand to supplies and services. Organizational hierarchies have become too expensive to sustain, and in many cases their style of coordination is simply no longer necessary. The cost complexity of the industrial complex starts to outweigh the benefits and the Internet is making it redundant.

"My expectation is that within five years this will have a major impact on the corporate organization. Jobs will be lost from the hierarchy and the jobs that remain will be very different. Instead of more ERP-supported supply chain management, employees, and eventually customers, will be the project managers of their own work – a concept that I call 'reality pull.' Big organizations only survive in a dynamic market by redesigning at least the organizational front-office into small autonomous units that can quickly react to volatile customer demand. Small cells can quickly respond to the market, but use the big corporate database and expertise.

They can combine the advantages of a big company with the advantages of a small company .

"This is where corporate social networking enters the picture. Of course, Twitter and Twitter lookalikes such as Yammer are not only tools. They are open source means to make the world much more transparent in terms of knowledge transfer and finding those with like interests. They allow you and me at an even lower price to find our peers, enlarging our ability to pool, ally and link, thereby enhancing our capability to create goal-oriented communities, networked organizations and focused action. Moreover, tools like Twitter allow for 'the real time Internet,' beating search engines by days in terms of quick, real time response capabilities.

"P2P banking, like Zopa or Smava, may serve as an example for this development toward social companies. An example for the real-time Internet, for traditional newspapers Twitter may serve as a new and cheap alert system for breaking news for their subscribers: just post a tweet.

"What is then the basic shift companies have to make to become a viable 21st century company? My guess is that where cooperation in the 20th century basically is a non-personal top-down, management driven calculation ('scientific management'), it will evolve into a bottom-up personal decision.

> *Lean and mean* will become *lean and meaningful.*

"The game will no longer be about schedule push mass solutions but about reality pull, personalized solutions. The non-personal top-down planning and strategy approach will be at least partially replaced by personal and continuous prototyping and 'perpetual beta,' thereby each of us turning into an action driven entrepreneur of our own talents and forcing us to leave our safe job titles.

"More and more companies will not be focused on continuity but on flexibility. Many companies will therefore have the character of temporary projects, creatively destructing themselves.

"Corporate social networking facilitates and accelerates this development toward a value-based network-centric attitude. It will force companies to become even more networked and therefore more human centered as this cooperative attitude fiercely reduces business operating cost. Current big companies, the corporates, will probably in the short run evolve into financial holdings, enabling 21st century human-centered social companies." [2]

The business implications of social media are profound and reveal why companies must become *lean and meaningful.*

Rearranging the Furniture for the Cloud Era

A different approach is needed to assemble and deploy Services in the Cloud era involving a rearrangement of players. Just ask the following question. Of both products and services, what would the delivery elements be in the Cloud? Let's use the diagram below to arrange our ideas and thoughts. Keep in mind that the diagram shows but one of multiple (or theoretically infinite) numbers of "triangles" supporting multiple individual users standing on the common base of Cloud delivery.

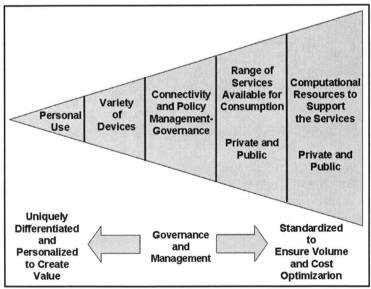

Delivery Elements in the Cloud for One or Any Number of Users

If we start on the left side of the diagram, then we know that at a personal level of use, we increasingly want to "have it our way." Think of the Apple iPhone for the selection of services we want to use, and cross that with a corporate thin client for the core enterprise services as new renderings of existing enterprise applications. The first change is that we will have to get out of calling people "users." Instead they are "consumers," selecting the services that are the best fit for their individual needs. There will be competition and dynamics in what will be consumed rather than imposed by some enterprise business intelligence package.

However, that does not mean the existing enterprise applications rendered as Services will die away The layer of enterprise transaction recording, procedures, shared data and so on definitely have to remain in place. As before with each new generation of technology, "Personal Use" just represents a new layer with different capabilities being added to the mix. In this case, the different capabilities focus on maximizing external business options around events and activities.

The diagram shows Personal Use as a narrow point because every consumer (user) will be different in his or her selection and use of Services to augment enterprise-defined Services to create value. However, this won't all be on a PC as we discussed in the previous section; there will be a variety of devices. So the question is not only how to deliver Services to these different kinds of devices but how the enterprise can provide the management controls on what can be delivered to which device, and what can be actively done from each device. That leads to the third layer of connectivity and policy management, which is the real challenge, and points to a whole new market for "system integrators cum outsourcers" and an emerging new breed of Cloud Brokerage firms that provide the needed policy management and governance services.

The range of available Services comes from a full spectrum of sources. Some may be provided by secure internal sources running on private Clouds. Others may be available as services that are consumed for a fee, the equivalent of SaaS vendors such as salesforce.com. All major software vendors will be using some form of SaaS model to deliver at least some part of their capabilities. Other services might be free, or at least supported by advertising. Google Maps is an example. Finally, the last layer in the diagram represents the computational resources needed to support the services. In this layer, standardization is everything.

The big new *integration* issue is focused on exactly how the two ends are connected. One end is focused on huge numbers of individuals. The other end is focused on huge-capacity resources.

It's not just the ability to provide the connections between these layers as each enterprise will no doubt maintain rules as to what services can be run on which devices. Then there are issues of who-did-what-with-whom and which Services are needed for governance and compliance—and that's before we get to who-pays-whom-for-what questions.

Open standards reduce integration work as long as we are talking about a one-dimensional IT model based on simple technology integration. On the other hand, the integration market for Services in the Cloud is only just beginning to become clear. Because enterprises want to maintain their focus on core businesses challenges, this looks to be a new market for systems integrators, now christened as Services Integrators and Cloud Brokerage firms.

Takeaway

Let's summarize the shift from Information Technology (IT) to Business Technology (BT) with a graphic:

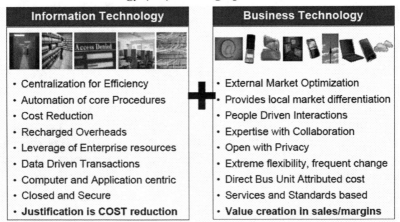

Information Technology	Business Technology
• Centralization for Efficiency	• External Market Optimization
• Automation of core Procedures	• Provides local market differentiation
• Cost Reduction	• People Driven Interactions
• Recharged Overheads	• Expertise with Collaboration
• Leverage of Enterprise resources	• Open with Privacy
• Data Driven Transactions	• Extreme flexibility, frequent change
• Computer and Application centric	• Direct Bus Unit Attributed cost
• Closed and Secure	• Services and Standards based
• **Justification is COST reduction**	• **Value creation in sales/margins**

From Information Technology (IT) to Business Technology (BT)

The following diagram from Forrester Research provides a quick summary of the evolution to Business Technology.

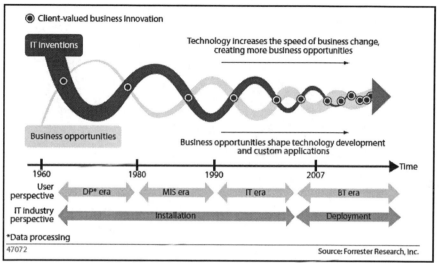

The Evolution to Business Technology

The key to Business Technology isn't cloud *computing*, it's cloud *services*.

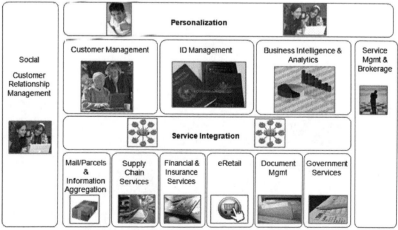

Cloud Services Everywhere, Anytime, All the Time

References.

[1] Adapted from http://www.youtube.com/watch?v=off08As3siM,
http://www.sti2.org/

[2] http://somesso.com/blog/2009/06/guest-article-frans-van-der-reep-on-social-companies

5. The Service-Oriented Enterprise in the Cloud

Key Points: What Does a Cloud-Powered Enterprise Look Like?

The organization that wants to win in the Participatory Society will become a Service-Oriented Enterprise (SOE). The emergence of never-before-available network bandwidth has enabled a transformation to a new services-oriented technology infrastructure. But even more significant, it has enabled the transformation to an enterprise of another kind.

The Cloud isn't just about data center consolidations and pay-per-drink cost savings, it's about transforming an enterprise to become a Service-Oriented Enterprise. In this chapter we explore the characteristics of a SOE and lay out strategies for migrating to this powerful form of business organization.

Before we start, let's clear up the confusion between using the term "Services" to indicate a technology element and approach versus using the term to mean the offerings that a business makes to its market and clients.

In our discussions, when you see the term Services, think "units of business" not "units of technology."

"Cloud computing" is about technology.

"Cloud Services" are intrinsically linked to the concept of providing a capability of use and value to a consumer.

The term Service-Oriented Architecture (SOA) looks very different when driven by the need to support flexible front office activities by using Services rather than when looked at as a possible way to carry out back office data-centric application integration.

There is a huge difference between IT developing centralized capabilities for cost efficiency that is budgeted as a back office overhead item, and the decentralization of front office capabilities around the edge of a business to optimize marketplace effectiveness. The front office goal is differentiation that creates value in terms of revenues and market share. In the front office, budgets and costs must be directly attributed to rapidly changing activities and available on demand, hence the pay-as-you-go Cloud services model.

Business Faces Pressing Issues

Have you tried to introduce a multichannel strategy for your company but discovered you didn't have the flexibility to make it happen? Would you like to establish an effective link between your enterprise portals and your back office so your online systems don't crash? Are you looking for a way to free up budgets that can be devoted to driving innovation within your organization?

If you answered "yes" to these questions it's time to turn your business into a Service-Oriented Enterprise (SOE).

Businesses today face a wide range of issues that impede growth and profitability. Chief among them is the need for greater flexibility, driven by factors such as multichannel strategies, pressure to improve time to market, and the impact of mergers and acquisitions. In particular, many businesses have failed to effectively integrate their Web-based channels and connect them to their legacy systems. The result is that online systems frequently crash with high visibility to the public, clients and competitors.

At the same time, companies are striving for adaptive cross-functional processes that can connect the silos created by their legacy enterprise systems (ERP, CRM, SCM and so on), while reducing unsupportable dependencies and costs. Today many companies' systems are linked together with an increasing amount of "spaghetti code." The result is that too much of the IT budget is devoted to maintaining existing capabilities and staffing to support legacy systems, leaving little room for innovation and investment in the future.

But times are changing, and opportunities are changing too. The tools are available today to help companies achieve greater adaptability, flexibility and collaboration. For one thing, open standards have become a reality. They are developing rapidly and have the support of the technology industry. In addition, open source has become mainstream as a method for sharing common software and is an element in software license reform. Open source software ensures that everyone can understand what they are seeing, as well as make a contribution. As a result, services are accessible through the Web with no restrictions on users or processors.

At the same time that companies struggled with the issues that plagued them, the technology industry began evolving and offering new solutions to address these challenges. The first Web Services (WS) technologies became available in 2000 but were wrought with interoperability problems. Extended Enterprise Projects followed, but they too faced difficulties with interoperability.

As these problems were worked out, integration projects began to move to Web Services while Enterprise Service Bus (ESB) technology vendors started appearing on the technology scene. By 2003, WS technology was exploding, even becoming mandated in some organizations. In recent years the Business Process Execution Language (BPEL) for WS began making headway, resulting in Application Platform Suites that could offer end-to-end service development. This has led to widespread adoption of Web Services and the standardization on BPEL for processes. Finally, today many of the technology vendors have moved to a Service-Oriented Architecture (SOA) approach and standards have begun to deal with Service Management and Operations.

These developments underpin the move toward increased Web use by providing the type of software and functionality that organizations require. In fact, as the Web rapidly moves into business technology in the same way it now dominates home technology, it is essential to developing integrated end-to-end processes that lie at the heart of a Service-Oriented Enterprise.

A constant trend in software development has been to "isolate" logical layers for increased flexibility and enhanced productivity (for example, data access and network transactions). Today, this can be achieved at a "services" level, which represents a step change in the industry based on the lessons of the Web. Yet the technologies and standards supporting it have been "cooking" for years. And this is precisely where cloud computing comes in as the "delivery mechanism" that accelerates the adoption of the Internet as the "mother of all services."

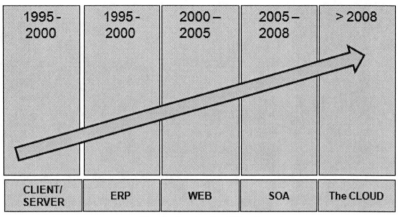

1995 - 2000	1995 - 2000	2000 - 2005	2005 - 2008	> 2008
CLIENT/ SERVER	ERP	WEB	SOA	The CLOUD

Evolution to the Cloud

In short, the key elements for a SOE transformation are in place right now:

- The business issues are pressing.
- Early adopters have shown the way.
- Mainstream technology vendors are coming into the market with products that build on and legitimize current investments.
- The community of enterprises and individuals at all levels is building to allow real open business.
- And, as important as any other factor,

> ... the SOE offers a way to turn expenditures on compliance from a cost drain to a means of delivering real business advantage.

Why Is SOE Compelling?

To understand the value created by a Service-Oriented Enterprise consider the business model of a traditional airline compared with that of a low-cost airline. Today's low-cost airlines offer consumers the ultimate in speed and flexibility. You can book when you choose, well ahead or at the last minute, at any time of day or night. Book early and the price will be low since demand is low; book late and demand may be high, so the price will be high. The converse may also be true. The airline has the flexibility to lower the price to sell off any oversupply of seats that remain at the last minute.

It's all about dynamic pricing and a different kind of business model. That model is based on an integrated set of end-to-end processes that connect the customer's needs to the company's internal processes without centralized dependencies. It's also about an open business model that provides visibility to buyers and sellers of all crucial information that can affect the decisions of both parties. And it makes this information available through the open technology of the Internet. The result for a customer is choice, speed, flexibility and satisfaction.

In contrast, most traditional airlines still operate on a silo model, where specialized applications are used to automate manual processes with no end-to-end integration. Compared to the horizontal processes and open interactions and transactions of the low-cost airlines, traditional airlines rely on a sequential, disconnected series of vertical functional silos supporting applications. The result for a customer is limited options, logjams and frustration.

By redesigning and automating processes driven by organizational and customer requirements, low-cost airlines provide choice, flexibility and scalability. This market-driven, Service-Oriented Enterprise model has allowed the low-cost airlines to expand rapidly, taking share from existing airlines as well as creating a bigger overall market. In comparison, many traditional airlines face declining market share, loss of profits and in some cases bankruptcy filings. *Which business model would you prefer to base your company's future on?*

Success today and in the years ahead, for airlines and all businesses, demands that a company transform itself into a Service-Oriented Enterprise. What really differentiates an SOE from a traditional business model is its "outside-in" approach. A SOE creates business-driven value by defining and exposing its core business processes to the external market through the use of standardized open technology in the form of "services." This reorganization includes new business requirements, new operating zones and new license structures, which can enable improved collaboration between organizations and their customers and suppliers. A

SOE has the capability to organize its responses to market shifts due to the agility within its culture, processes and IT systems.

> What really differentiates a SOE from
> a traditional business model is its "outside-in" approach.

By building on its adaptive and agile investments internally, a company can take advantage of increasing external capabilities for interactive communication. This allows for improved collaboration with business partners by using services to reach the optimum decision in response to events. The value created from a Service-Oriented Enterprise is manifested in three key capability areas:

- *Sense and Respond:* All customer-facing processes and people are engaged in a collaborative development process based on real-life situations. This capability allows companies to develop real-time marketing and dynamic pricing based on access to actual customer dialogs and transactions. The technology foundation enables this capability by synthesizing the massive flow of data into instructions and shared best practices.

- *Plug and Play:* Open standards enable rapid adoption of best practices and integration with a company's alliance ecosystem. This results in scalability and flexibility through a services approach to customer needs. A company is thus able to adapt its response to the current situation. This capability is enabled through Service-Oriented Architecture and Service-Oriented Infrastructure.

- *Learn and Leverage:* New capabilities enable new business models in new markets, channels and geographies. Customer participation is incorporated into the offer development, marketing and delivery. This allows for rapid prototyping, which can then be ramped up or discarded as appropriate through Service-Oriented Architecture. The technology driving this includes interoperable technical, semantic and legal capabilities in the company's ecosystem.

What Is a SOE and What Does It Look Like?

At its core, a Service-Oriented Enterprise is all about reorganizing the enterprise to enable increased collaboration between the company and its customers, suppliers and other trading partners. From this collaboration will come greater efficiency, faster time-to-market, reduced costs, and improved flexibility and responsiveness—the hallmarks of a Service-Oriented Enterprise.

> A SOE is able to change its capability mix quickly
> and efficiently, and on a fine-grained scale,
> to continually optimize the business.

To accomplish this means changing from a "silo capability model" to a "market capability model," a shift that has been under way for some years now. Non-core activities are being shed in the drive for true focus, but the disposals have mostly been in the form of slow, large-scale change ("Maybe we should let someone else run our IT infrastructure and call centers"). They have not come in the form of dynamic process adjustments in response to a specific market opportunity ("Let's launch this new line extension in Eastern Europe together with our German distributor using a third-party order management and delivery partner").

A SOE is able to change its capability mix quickly and efficiently, and on a fine-grained scale, to continually optimize the business. It's a cultural, managerial and IT issue in the same way that moving to more effective "matrix work" was a natural result of the shift to PC networked employees.

Supporting a SOE are four fundamental elements: sensor technology, Service-Oriented Infrastructure, Service-Oriented Architecture and business processes. These elements allow a business to build a process that leverages services in the Cloud.

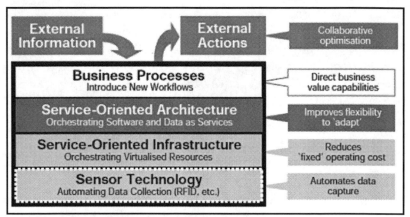

Supporting the Service-Oriented Enterprise

Most businesses today operate with a project-based integration approach. This approach is characterized by the use of native application technology and embedded data and process management. It also assumes little or no change, makes limited use of common resources and focuses on "big bang" application deployment projects. A project-based integration approach:

- Results in risk, cost and delays even for the first delivery
- Resists change
- Prevents a dynamic process-centric approach
- Precludes end-to-end process and information visibility

Is there a better way?
We believe so.

> Architecture is the key to bringing coherence
> to an organization and building a Service-Oriented Enterprise.

Enterprise architecture knocks down barriers and creates more open systems. It is characterized by an extensive reuse of common data and processes, a process-centric approach with supervisory process management, and an assumption of continuous change. The impact of this approach is significant. Enterprise architecture:

- Creates flexibility and responsiveness
- Supports incremental, evolutionary change
- Minimizes total cost of ownership (TCO)
- Maximizes information and process velocity

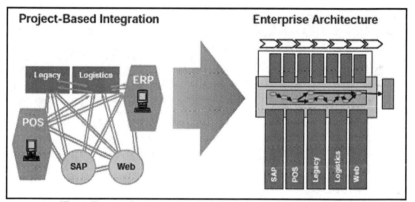

From Project-based Integration to Enterprise Architecture

The Cloud is the future. It provides almost infinite, flexible and scalable external computing and processing services that not only offer significant cost benefits, but also provide the ability to connect with customers, partners and suppliers like never before. However, without Service-Oriented Architecture (SOA), organizations will find it almost impossible to reach the cloud.

The Re-Birth of Service-Oriented Architecture (SOA)

Mention "IT architecture" and most business executives will excuse themselves and head for the door. Software architecture definition has long been an intuitive process with few formal procedures or notations. But today, the increasing rate of business and technological change is forcing companies to seriously examine the architecture of new systems.

In traditional IT architecture, computer applications were designed to handle specific business functions for specific business units, e.g., the invoicing application for the billing department. Services on the other hand are designed without knowing the uses they will be called on to support, e.g., Google maps used for finding a piece of real estate or finding the exact location of a restaurant. Traditional IT architecture works from the company's internal view of the outside world; it works from the inside-out.

Outside-in architecture starts with what is visible from outside, i.e., the way customers view the business. Starting with customer-facing business processes, we perform analysis and then move in toward creating services that are directly linked with the business requirements for serving customers.

The *outside-in* architectural style of Service-Oriented Architecture (SOA) *distributes* governance as a central architectural component. Thomas Winans and John Seely Brown observe, "Implementation of an outside-in architecture results in better architecture layering and factoring, and interfaces that become more business than data oriented. Policy becomes more explicit, and is exposed in a way that makes it easier to change it as necessary. Service orientation guides the implementation, making it more feasible to integrate and interoperate using a commodity infrastructure rather than using complex and inflexible application integration middleware."[1] The shift to an outside-in SOA architectural style is the cornerstone for transitioning from traditional IT architectures to Cloud-oriented architectures.

Service-Oriented Architecture is not new. Many companies are already using SOA and saving money as a result. What is new, however, is the notion of applying SOA across the entire enterprise in a coherent fashion in order to realize the full business benefits of a Service-Oriented Enterprise. As one CEO explained, "We have a lot of projects going on now where people are using Service-Oriented Architecture. The problem is that I'm pretty sure all of those will turn out to be incompatible and potentially explode on us." In fact, he is almost certainly right.

In a blog entry, enterprise architect Anne Thomas Manes exclaimed, "SOA is Dead; Long Live Services." "Obituary: SOA met its demise on January 1, 2009, when it was wiped out by the catastrophic impact of the economic recession. SOA is survived by its offspring: mashups, BPM, SaaS, Cloud Computing, and all other architectural approaches that depend on 'services.'

"Once thought to be the savior of IT, SOA instead turned into a great failed experiment—at least for most organizations. SOA was supposed to reduce costs and increase agility on a massive scale. Except in rare situations, SOA has failed to deliver its promised benefits. After investing millions, IT systems are no better than before. In many organizations, things are worse: costs are higher, projects take longer, and systems are more fragile than ever. The people holding the purse strings have had enough. With the tight budgets of 2009, most organizations have cut funding for their SOA initiatives.

"It's time to accept reality. SOA fatigue has turned into SOA disillusionment. Business people no longer believe that SOA will deliver spectacular benefits. 'SOA' has become a bad term. It must be removed from our vocabulary.

"The demise of SOA is tragic for the IT industry. Organizations desperately need to make architectural improvements to their application portfolios. Service-orientation is a prerequisite for rapid integration of data and business processes; it enables situational development models, such as mashups; and it's the foundational architecture for SaaS and cloud computing. (Imagine shifting aspects of your application portfolio to the cloud without enabling integration between on-premise and off-premise applications.) Although the term SOA is dead, the requirement for service-oriented architecture is stronger than ever.

"But perhaps that's the challenge: The acronym got in the way. People forgot what SOA stands for. They were too wrapped up in silly technology debates (e.g., What's the best ESB? or WS-* vs. REST), and they missed the important stuff—architecture and services.

"Successful SOA (i.e., application re-architecture) requires disruption to the status quo. SOA is not simply a matter of deploying new technology and building service interfaces to existing applications; it requires redesign of the application portfolio. And it requires a massive shift in the way IT operates. The small select group of organizations that has seen spectacular gains from SOA did so by treating it as an agent of transformation. In each of these success stories, SOA was just one aspect of the transformation effort. And here's the secret to success: SOA needs to be part of something bigger. If it isn't, then you need to ask yourself why you've been doing it.

"The latest shiny new technology will not make things better. Incremental integration projects will not lead to significantly reduced costs and increased agility. If you want spectacular gains, then you need to make a spectacular commitment to change. Like Bechtel. It's interesting that the Bechtel story [Bechtel ventured into the cloud, benchmarking itself against Google, Amazon, Salesforce.com and YouTube to gain insight into how it could reduce costs and improve performance in the areas of server management, storage, application management and network costs. See link in references for "The Google-ization of Bechtel"] [2] doesn't even use the term SOA—it just talks about services.

"And that's where we need to concentrate from this point forward: Services." [3]

With regard to the complexity encountered when using SOA as a substitute for EAI in application integration, many analysts have concluded that "SOA is dead." In contrast, Randy Heffner at Forrester produced research that updates the casual market view of SOA with a much more in-depth study under the title, "SOA Is Far From Dead, But It Should Be Buried." Randy's point is that SOA is part of a much larger technology change and should be seen as part of this, not as a standalone solution. Therefore, it should be buried in the much larger issue of delivering Cloud, Web 2.0 and collaboration-based solutions.

The disappointing results from early SOA projects was a result of lack of coordination and direction. Consider what happened in the case of the rampant process reengineering that took place in the 1990s. Enthusiastic business unit leaders achieved great improvements in individual processes. Yet the transformation programs and enabling technologies were usually not robust enough to create lasting change across the entire enterprise, not to mention between the enterprise and its customers and trading partners.

All too often the reality is that using SOA is merely a substitute for Enterprise Application Integration (EAI). You might hear the CIO say, "Yes we can do EAI with SOA, but there is so much custom work that the claimed benefits for reuse are actually very difficult to achieve." There's certainly something to agree with in this statement because the actual work being performed is one-to-one application integration. But if we look at the core principles of SOA it represents a paradigm for both Business and IT architecture. That's a really important point to grasp. "Services" must be defined as "units of business," not "units of technology," else we are indeed limited to IT architecture and EAI alone.

If you look at the world of IT built around applications, then architecture is focused on the technical computing system elements. From this perspective the job is to understand which, where, and how the various technical elements have to be integrated. Sure there are business requirements driving this, but the expertise and focus is largely on the technology aspects.

Now think about Business Technology and the fast-changing front office world using Web 2.0 and the Cloud. It's not the same thing at all. For a start it's not based on monolithic stateful applications. It's based on clusters of business Services, meaning small self-contained *business* tasks or functions.

If you work your way through the attributes, then pretty well everything about a Services environment is a reversal of an application environment—Stateful vs. Stateless; Tightly Coupled vs. Loosely Coupled; Deterministic vs. non Deterministic and so on. In general, Applications are first and foremost all about transactional data, whereas Services are all about flexible processes, and there well may be no transactional data involved. This explains the Business Architecture notion that business managers want the ability to change and vary their front office processes frequently in response to external conditions. Conversely IT Architects must control change to ensure the stability of the transactional procedures and systems of record. Because these are two very different goals it's not surprising that they are not always seen together.

SOA also becomes critical as the mechanism to link the two environments. If you are not using Services or providing front office support then you probably have a fair argument to say that SOA is not providing any real value to your organization. When focused on the front office, SOA enables a business to change its processes and achieve competitive differentiation. Take the example of Dell. While its products and services may not be significantly different, its outside-in approach to business architecture is its competitive differentiator.

In 2009, Gartner analysts proclaimed that it's time to embrace a new architecture. A new style of enterprise architecture is required to respond to increased complexities in today's markets, economies, nations, networks and companies. The firm's analysts are now advising companies to adopt "emergent architecture," also known as middle-out and light enterprise architecture, as business units demand more autonomy. The idea behind it is that organizations have very little control over what individuals within the enterprise are doing, and it emphasizes the innovation that can happen throughout a business from the bottom up.

1. Accessibility: The cloud is accessible through a SOA interface
2. Visibility: SOA tools and techniques can help an organization find services that meet its needs
3. Extensibility: Cloud services can be modified and customized using SOA techniques
4. Matching Expectations: Cloud services require clear SLAs; deploy these using SOA contract-management techniques
5. Adherence to Standards: SOA policy management techniques validate that an organization follow appropriate cloud standards

Five Reasons to Utilize SOA on the Way to the Cloud

"Many organizations operate under the assumption that everything can be standardized, but that is far from true," said Bruce

Robertson, V.P. of Research at Gartner. By adding an emergent aspect to enterprise architecture, you remove the top-down approach of central thinkers and, instead, let the innovation emerge among those doing the work. Gartner identified seven properties that differentiate emergent architecture from traditional enterprise architecture:

1. *Non-deterministic.* Emergent architecture decentralizes decision-making, enabling innovation.

2. *Autonomous actors.* Today's business environment no longer allows enterprise architects to control all aspects of architecture. Emergent architectures recognize the broader business ecosystem and transfer control to constituents.

3. *Rule-bound actors.* In the past, enterprise architects provided detailed design specifications for all aspects of the enterprise. Emergent calls for a defined set of rules and enables choice.

4. *Goal-oriented actors.* Each constituent should act in their own best interests, rather than a singular focus on the corporate.

5. *Local influences.* Enterprise architects must increasingly coordinate efforts because actors are increasingly influenced by local interactions and have limited information. Feedback within their sphere of communication alters individual behavior.

6. *Dynamic or adaptive systems.* The system (the individual actors as well as the environment) changes over time. Enterprise architecture must design emergent systems and respond to changes in their environment.

7. *Resource-constrained environment.* An environment of abundance does not enable emergence; rather, the scarcity of resources drives emergence.

A Service-Oriented Architecture is enabled by a Service-Oriented Infrastructure (SOI). SOI is the infrastructure operated by the IT Services department that provides a common and shared set of technologies that enable the business processes to be added and changed readily. SOI can also reduce the cost and complexity of operating these services and existing legacy applications. With SOI, design and management changes to meet dynamic business demand for flexibility, cost efficiency and quality of service.

A traditional IT infrastructure is application driven. Resources are dedicated to applications and there is a high degree of client-owned assets. Traditional infrastructure is generally unable to share spare capacity and its support costs are a burden on available capital. As a result, a business has difficulty reacting to change or demand, little scope for innovation or cost reduction, and a lack of process flexibility.

By comparison, a Service-Oriented Infrastructure is service driven. With a SOI, virtualization slashes support costs by pooling expensive processors and other infrastructure items. This also results in increased utilization and reduced capital costs. Additional characteristics of SOI include:

- Process area network, which meets demand peaks
- Auditable configuration for compliance
- Content-addressable storage
- Converged voice and data
- Deep packet analysis network intelligence
- Device and service interoperation

What's required today is a fundamental change in the approach to provisioning and managing a SOI. Virtualization and distributed delivery become the keys to delivering access to processing and storage capabilities provided in the form of services. Coupled with radical improvements in automation technology, the short-term impact on infrastructure design and management is substantial, but so is the payoff in cost savings and performance.

While Infrastructure as a Service (IaaS) has come into use for provisioning raw computing resources, much of this needs to be based on Platform as a Service (PaaS) onto which Software as a Service (SaaS) can be rapidly implemented and orchestrated via BPM as a Service (BPMaaS). In short, a powerful Service-Oriented Infrastructure is a Cloud-oriented Infrastructure.

> SOA allows a business to change its processes
> and radically improve its ability to service the market.

A critical aspect of a Service-Oriented Enterprise is the effective deployment of cloud computing to enable technological change itself. But even more important is support for enterprise transformation. Winners and losers will be determined by their ability to design and manage increasingly open, virtualized and dynamic environments.

We'll explore more about the critical subject of Enterprise Architecture and another key to enterprise cloud computing, Process-Oriented Architecture (POA) in Chapter 7, "Enterprise Cloud Computing: The Process."

What the Transformation Opportunity Looks Like

Moving from a Service-Oriented Enterprise theory to reality requires that a company set enterprise goals and directions and link existing investments around a Service-Oriented Infrastructure and Service-Oriented Architecture. This approach will demand an external focus and education.

Where do you start? The simple answer is to find the key processes that can differentiate your business on both the buying and selling sides.

Take a look at the *edge* of your enterprise, where the characteristics of regular change in support of a key process occur. An alternative is to start by identifying process domains that are clearly dysfunctional or uncompetitive—typically in comparison to new market entrants who have been able to start from scratch. Use the capabilities embedded in a SOA to rapidly build these new capabilities into your processes, systems and people. This can help you set new goals for business definitions and technology delivery as well as measurable metrics for new definitions of success.

Equally important are the longer-term benefits that stem from the new cost structure inherent in a service-based environment.

> The cost savings from using SOI and SOA
> create the headroom for innovation and investment
> —the critical factors for future growth.

The Dynamics of the Business Transformation

All companies can benefit from becoming a Service-Oriented Enterprise. However, the way in which different businesses engage the market and the benefits they derive will vary depending on the maturity of the enterprise and the industry.

In the case of a new player in a mature industry, the SOE approach allows a business to do what it does, but cheaper and more effectively. By building a SOE platform from scratch, and leveraging "virtual" alliances via the Cloud, these types of companies can break through the existing process paradigms of their industry.

In contrast, an established player in a mature industry can take a more evolutionary SOE approach by gradually replacing processes to achieve a cost and scale advantage. In this case, a business would select sub-processes in specific lines of business and geographies for SOE migration, and extend and integrate those on a "proof-of-return" basis.

For a new player in an emerging industry, a SOE offers the potential to innovate faster than the competition. A SOE helps the company stay closer to its customers in order to change as they change, based on a fully service-oriented platform. In other words, the business becomes totally adaptive.

In the case of an established player entering an emerging industry a SOE provides the ability to release the "new" from the legacies of the "old." A company can configure new lines of business for start-up opportunities on "pure" SOE platforms while interfacing with legacy systems to push change toward the center.

As with all technology-enabled business change, a critical success factor in the transformation of a business to a Service-Oriented Enterprise will be the ability to train and motivate people to respond to challenges beyond their own narrow band of responsibility. Going back to our earlier airline example, consider that pilots at many of the low-cost airlines also supervise—and sometimes even help with—loading and unloading baggage. Most people react positively to the opportunity to broaden their participation in the enterprise's value chain, but only if they can see the alignment of the enterprise objectives with their own personal growth and success.

Startups and Legacy Players

Making the shift to a SOE will only succeed with leadership that can transcend the time-tested silo models. It is this traditional functional or departmental focus that is so often the root cause of the friction that keeps large organizations from responding swiftly to new market situations. For an enterprise to become a SOE requires a transformational journey that must be configured, planned and navigated with the full participation of senior leaders. It will not be a quick fix; no silver bullets. But with appropriate methodologies there will be significant short-term and long-term benefits from a Service-Oriented Enterprise to mitigate the necessary investments in people, processes and technologies.

> As with so many transformational changes,
> making the shift to a SOE will only succeed
> with leadership that can transcend time-tested silo models.

Takeaway: How to Deliver the SOE Collaboratively

Rather than the typical "big bang" program where an entire division or enterprise is scrutinized and laboriously changed over a period of months or years (often to find that the business realities have changed when the transformation is finished), a SOE takes a far more "surgical" approach. The existing investments in IT stay in place, but now it's about how a company uses them better to support market-driven business processes. A SOE approach allows a business to target with surgical precision how and where to make a difference without disturbing every other part of the enterprise.

Leading technology companies are shaping the industry direction for creating a SOE in order to help business make this shift from "big to small." Collaboration is the key to meeting the SOE challenge and to developing a changed understanding, culture and approach that redefines the enterprise as truly being "Open for Business."

Taking a collaborative approach may not be typical for many businesses, but it is an essential aspect of building a SOE. Collaboration should serve as the framework of common aim and direction that drives a SOE.

The Service-Oriented Enterprise understands the importance of using standards to conduct business. Imagine where the Web would be if Web servers and browsers didn't follow universal standards. If your company works with technology consulting firms or systems integrators, make sure they are committed to open standards. Even more, your technology providers should also be significant contributors to open source initiatives and work with standards organizations such as the Object Management Group (OMG), Organization for the Advancement of Structured Information Standards (OASIS), and The Open Group to develop implementation standards for SOA. Like business itself, standards evolve and so your technology partners must stay involved with the appropriate standards organizations.

For today's enterprise, the message is clear. Service-Oriented Architecture and the Cloud are here now, and companies need to act on these new realities. Organizations that do not deploy SOA and attempt to take advantage of the Cloud will face a serious risk of being outperformed by their competitors who do.

References.

[1] Winans, Thomas and John Seely Brown, "Moving information technology platforms to the clouds — Insights into IT platform architecture transformation," White Paper, April 2009.

[2] "The Google-ization of Bechtel" http://www.networkworld.com/news/2008/102908-bechtel.html

[3] http://apsblog.burtongroup.com/2009/01/soa-is-dead-long-live-services.html

6. Business Process Management (BPM) in the Cloud

"There is nothing permanent except change."
—Heraclitus 6th Century BC.

Key Points: The Process-Driven Enterprise.

The Service-Oriented Enterprise is the Process-Driven Enterprise, and it's Business Process Management (BPM) that gives the enterprise the agility it needs to innovate and thrive. This is at the heart of the concept of Business Technology mentioned earlier, where business people can take direct control of their business processes. As we've discussed, it's the front office customer-facing processes that count for business advantage, not the back office recordkeeping and internal administrative processes.

The way the business operates, the way it does things, needs to be reexamined. That means that a company's business processes must be well understood, thorough and yet quickly adaptable. It's no longer just *what* you do that counts, it's *how* you do what you do – and how quickly you can modify your business processes to take on new opportunities and challenges – that's really important.

Change and the Organization

Another well known saying attributed to Heraclitus was that "Everything flows, nothing stands still." Sadly that is hardly true of the modern organization and to understand why we must look at the organization in greater detail. At an abstract level we can simplify the structure of an organization and view it as having three basic components: Strategy, Organization and Infrastructure. Looking at an organization in this way quickly tells us that to get maximum value from the deployed assets we have to understand the very different dynamics of each layer:

- *Strategy:* The strategy is set at the highest level of the organization and typically changes between 1 to 2 years.
- *Organization:* The organization is typically in a state of flux and changes every 3 to 6 months. It is the responsibility of the organization to execute on the strategy.
- *Infrastructure:* In this context we are talking about company's property, plant and equipment, its offices, its networks and its information technology. One could argue that this infrastructure rate of change is much slower than the rest of the organization. On average, the infrastructure changes between 6 and 10 years. In fact, the last great change in infrastructure was when we were faced with the millennium or Y2K bug scare.

A Service-Oriented Enterprise helps us manage the demands of these seemingly conflicting layers. Given that the dynamics of change are out of synch we need to understand what impact that has on our ability to respond to changing market dynamics. The enterprise will have had at least three strategy life cycles to one infrastructure life cycle.

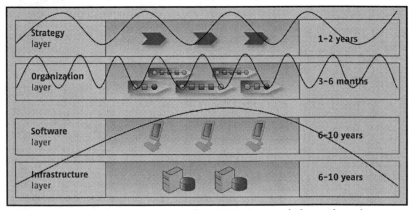

Companies can change strategy and organization much faster than they can change their software and hardware infrastructures

To align these core functions the organization needs to examine itself and the first port of call should be its *business processes*, that is, how it gets its work done to provide value to its customers.

Unfortunately, many studies and surveys show that changes to IT infrastructure and applications are fraught with complexity, costing much more and taking much longer than initially anticipated. It is not uncommon for an IT organization to take five or more years to make significant enterprise-wide changes. This pace just doesn't provide the speed at which business initiatives must be implemented in today's business climate.

Another issue straining relationships between business and IT is the difficulty in finding common ground for the communication between them. Business people often have poor understanding of existing business processes that they wish to improve and little to no visibility into how effective these processes actually are. They also often lack sufficient technical expertise to specify their requirements in a structured manner that would ensure they are complete, consistent and accurate.

As a result, IT implementations often do not deliver exactly what was required by the business, and consequently lengthy and expensive rework is needed. Rather than supporting business agility, this communication conundrum between business and IT becomes a kind of quicksand in the way of progress—not to mention a source of conflict between business and IT professionals.

This constant friction between the business desire to achieve a rapid pace of change and the ability of IT to deliver it resulted in what is infamously known as the "Business-IT Gap." Instead of being in a position to help the business to become more competitive, IT has to invest most of its budget in maintenance of existing legacy systems and applications.

The Emergence of Business Process Management Systems

A key solution that helps organizations become more efficient and agile is the Business Process Management System (BPMS). The BPMS is a set of tools designed to help businesses discover how their processes work and how to measure, manage and optimize them. Properly implemented, a BPMS helps organizations to pin-point and resolve process bottlenecks, monitor and anticipate business activity and quickly react to the constantly changing business environment. Many industry analysts recognize the BPMS as one of the most important enterprise software market segments, and it is not surprising to find many vendors attempting to address the growing demand.

Unfortunately, most current offerings fall short of delivering the full promise of business process management. A good way to put this failure in context is to take a look at how "first generation" BPMS offerings have evolved out of two important technology segments: workflow automation and Enterprise Application Integration (EAI).

Workflow solutions have been around for a long time, and are primarily used for the routing of tasks and documents among individuals or groups based on a prescribed set of process flows, as well as collecting required information from the participants using structured forms. While adequate as simple routing tools, in the context of process management, workflow automation products have major shortcomings:

- They do not easily facilitate system-to-system or human-to-system integration and messaging.
- They are bound to prescribed processes that deal with very predictable and well defined activities. Conceptually, they are not built around the concepts of constant and rapid change with required support for dynamic self-changing processes.
- They are typically based on client-server architectures rather than modern architectural concepts such as Service-Oriented Architecture (SOA), Web services and thin clients.
- Most are implemented using outdated programming languages and represent processes in proprietary notation rather than industry-standard XML-based notations.
- Because of their older architectures and implementation approaches, they typically cannot support collaboration across multiple companies.

BPMS suites also grew out of EAI offerings, which provide a set of tools to facilitate and orchestrate the flow of data, operations and transactions across heterogeneous enterprise systems and applications. In the process management context, these products have major limitations:

- They focus on system-level, short-lived, transaction-oriented processes, and rarely support tasks and operations that are performed by people as part of an overarching business process.
- They are focused on the needs of IT, and are very technical platforms that require significant expertise to deploy.
- As a result, they provide very little value to business people as they offer little if any visibility and control at the business level.

Most workflow vendors recognized the severe limitations of their offerings, and have attempted to overcome these limitations mostly by developing new functional layers, as well as partnering or incorporating third-party products to complement their basic platforms. Similarly, most EAI vendors recognized the inherent deficiencies of their platforms and attempted to combine them with workflow systems to deliver a more holistic process approach capable of supporting business processes that span both systems and people. Internal development, partnerships or acquisitions have been the most common approaches for augmenting EAI products for the process management context.

Unfortunately, attempts to create a credible BPM solution by stitching together workflow and EAI technologies often yield very poor results. From the business user point of view, there are multiple reasons for this:

- Interaction between business and IT professional is still disconnected. Process models are being worked on by business people in a separate environment, and their transition to implementation and deployment by IT is risky and error-prone. This means that the business cannot be assured prior to deployment that what was required actually got implemented. It also means that process documentation and process implementation are often not synchronized.
- There is no single process-centric view that helps the business to monitor and resolve problems in the context of the process as they designed it. In short, first generation BPM platforms have separate and disconnected implementation models for "design time" processes and operational "run-time" processes.

This separation is artificial and significantly reduces the appeal of the BPM value proposition. It makes it much harder to provide truly "closed loop" BPM, in which processes are iteratively designed, developed, deployed, monitored and improved over time.

- Being still based on client-server models and "monolithic" architectures rather than on Internet-based distribution and modular designs, these systems tend to exhibit rigidity and "resist" rapid changes. Worse, they typically have inferior support for processes that go beyond organizational boundaries. This shortcoming is unacceptable in today's globalized business environment.

- Such systems often result in several "specialized" servers and repositories, which are integrated in the context of the overall solution. Such separation of servers frequently results in high total cost of ownership: high software, hardware, deployment and administration expenses for these complex, "integrated" configurations. The inevitable outcome: longer time-to-value.

These and other problems have significant adverse impacts on the ROI and success probability of deploying first-generation BPM solutions in a way that helps companies weather the storm and come out the other side leaner and fitter and better able to compete in a business world that has changed dramatically. Businesses can and should expect much more from their IT investments.

Next Generation BPM:
The Business Operations Platform

As the problematic nature of existing offerings became clear, a new generation of BPM solutions has emerged: the Business Operations Platform (BOP). But what makes it different from what's gone before?

The combination of the high availability of Cloud infrastructures at a low cost and innovative Cloud services means that the organization needs a *choreography* layer in the Cloud to fully deliver useful business advantages. Without this capability the Cloud is more likely to be used just to provide data center elasticity and

Software as a Service capabilities rather than a way to innovate and gain maximum advantage from technology. And that's precisely where business process management comes in.

Organizations that understand the benefits the Cloud realize that they have to create a *process layer* that decouples the control of business processes from underlying applications. In other words, process segments buried in traditional computer applications need to be rendered as "services," services that can be bundled, unbundled and rebundled as end-to-end business processes. In the same way that middleware provides a data abstraction layer, a Business Operations Platform provides a process abstraction layer that delivers business services when and where they are needed.

In short, a BOP can help businesses deploy, execute, measure, manage and optimize their business processes in the Cloud. Properly implemented, a BOP can help organizations pin-point and resolve process bottlenecks, monitor and anticipate business activity and quickly react to the constantly changing business environment.

Many industry analysts recognize process technology as one of the most important software technologies needed for deploying effective Cloud solutions. There are two clear reasons for needing process technology to underpin the provisioning of business systems in the Cloud:

1. *Rapid Innovation:* As we have seen, the Cloud is the ideal mechanism for utilizing extensive computing power – be that storage or specific applications such as CRM, ERP or SCM. As it stands, running a given application in the Cloud, also known as Software as a Service (SaaS) saves money. But SaaS solutions don't help a business innovate as all companies using a SaaS application are using the same software. SaaS solutions don't enable companies to build unique applications that differentiate them from their competitors. Process management technology, on the other hand, lets you do this in an easy and flexible way. A BOP can orchestrate the interaction and integration of services to create and manage unique business processes.

2. *Compliance:* Cloud deployments can be very disruptive and lead to anarchy and a breakdown of corporate governance and compliance. Think of the myriad of Excel spreadsheets that are

used to run most businesses—no control, no compliance, no ownership. Process enablement of these types of applications can provide ownership, control and auditability, making them compliant with the corporate governance demands without stifling innovation and change.

Before the BOP was available, enterprise applications typically would be in charge of their localized sets of processes with the subjugation of adjacent applications to these processes. With every application handling a given process differently, clearly this won't be a workable solution in the Cloud. With a BOP, the control of business processes is externalized away from individual applications. The BOP controls the execution of the processes, the provisioning of services and the delegation of tasks or activities to the individual applications according to their specific uses and needs. In order to do this effectively, the BOP must be able to support the following:

- Manage applications in parallel as well as in series.
- Manage people-intensive applications.
- Decouple the process from the application.
- Work both inside and outside the organization.
- Be both continuous and discrete, and allow processes to change over time.
- Put the control of business processes into the hands of the business user.

One of the key innovations (and there are many) is the *collaborative* nature of the platform. Finally there is an environment that allows, and encourages, the business world and the technology world to align. Given that the business process is where these two worlds come together, the BOP becomes the place where the two worlds can achieve the most in terms of collaborative development and common understanding—eliminating decades of misunderstanding. The Business Operations Platform does six main jobs:

1. It puts existing and new application software under the direct control of business managers.
2. It facilitates communication between business and IT.

3. It makes it easier for the business to improve existing processes and create new ones.
4. It enables the automation of processes across the entire organization—and beyond.
5. It gives managers real-time information on the performance of processes.
6. It allows organizations to take full advantage of new computing services.

Unlike early BPM offerings that were stitched together from fragments of technologies past, a BOP must be built on a standards-based, modern architecture. With service oriented architecture (SOA) and full BPM capabilities, companies can create a complete business operations environment that can drive innovation, efficiency and agility.

The BOP must include business process design, execution, monitoring and improvement capabilities. It must be designed to help business managers directly align business process implementations with business goals, while facilitating process improvement via control and visibility into process metrics and real-time business activity. At the same time, the BOP must help IT managers and developers to model and integrate the entire enterprise business process landscape, while ensuring that existing IT assets are fully leveraged.

The user interface should be completely Web based to make collaboration much easier, especially if business and IT professionals reside in multiple geographical locations. A shared process model defines the "contract" for process implementation, which is fulfilled by connecting top-down business process design components to bottom-up technical services. This approach puts the business firmly in charge by empowering business professionals to directly influence and control IT implementations. Furthermore, the BOP approach gives business managers and business analysts complete confidence that their models are up to date and reflect actual deployed processes.

On top of these capabilities, a BOP should also provide a Composite Application Framework (CAF) and enterprise Master

Data Management (MDM) to establish a single view of the business that can then be continuously and effectively monitored via the platform's integrated Business Activity Monitoring (BAM). This level of visibility makes continuous business process improvement a reality. It helps the organization to reach operational excellence via analysis of non-performing processes and reduction of process-related friction across the extended supply chain.

Finally, a BOP must enable comprehensive process auditing that helps decision makers to achieve better process governance. This is necessary to better comply with external and internal regulations and quality initiatives, such as SOX, Six Sigma, HIPAA, or Basel II. From an architectural perspective a BOP must be fully Cloud enabled and have ways of metering and monitoring what's happening and where it is happening. In short a BOP must be fully deployable in private, public and hybrid Clouds.

A Business Operations Platform Based on Shared Services

In summary, the Business Operations Platform is a fully integrated SOA and BPM platform designed to model, execute and monitor all types of workflows, including human-to-human workflows, system-to-system integration-type interactions and hybrid processes that involve both humans and systems. SOA layers enable IT to become more flexible and agile to meet business demands more effectively. A BOP can enable business professionals to gain better visibility over business processes, and to transition their requirements to IT with greater confidence.

Situational Applications: The Opportunity or the Threat for Business Technology

Situational Applications are applications quickly built for unique "situations" around the edge of the enterprise. The term was first coined as part of the movement toward "Agile Development." The term has moved back into the mainstream as part of the shift toward using "services" and "clouds" together with agile development to create high-value specialized capabilities for limited numbers of users extremely rapidly.

As technology becomes ubiquitously part of business, and an increasing number of users have a working knowledge of simple assembly style programming, then the use of unique localized capabilities will clearly rise. The challenge is where to allow this to happen versus where it would be dangerous and compromise the integrity of the enterprise and its systems. This is where complexity is low and requirements are limited, contained and unique. As such Situational Applications are frequently said to be the "Long Tail" of software use.

A useful comparison is to liken Situational Applications to spreadsheets in terms of being valuable tools for individuals and groups, but seldom do they have any integrated role in enterprise IT systems. Users can, and do, construct their own spreadsheets to solve a wide variety of unique localized needs without needing any professional programming help. In the same way, Situational Applications are normally provided as platforms that are self contained and designed for business users to be able to create a complete solution for their needs.

The IT department is torn between two different issues. On one hand the value to an enterprise could be very high. Situational Applications could unload back to business users a growing burden on IT staff for support services. On the other hand, this could result in an uncontrollable spread of unauditable applications that could endanger the integrity of enterprise applications overall. Ignoring these issues will not work, as users are perfectly able to build Situational Applications without the IT department having any knowledge of their activities. Best practice is to introduce tools and methods that can provide auditability.

The checklist from Jonathan Sapir's book, *Power in the Cloud: Using Cloud Computing to Build Information Systems at the Edge of Chaos*, can be used to ensure that the choice to use a Situational Application is well matched to what it can deliver, and to stress an understanding of the differences from traditional IT development.

	Traditional App. Development	*Situational App. Development*
Stake holders	IT Dept & Business Managers	Self-organizing user community
Targeted users	Large generic department or group	Limited to the small initiation community
Governance	Centralized and formalized routines	Community responsibility for controlled use
Evolutions	Top down, centrally driven and funded	Organic, user participation no formal funds
Time to Value	Months, possibly in large programs years	Days or a few weeks to value
Development phases	Defined project timetable and phases	Iterative and continuous from users
Functional requirements	Mgt defined, frozen delivery, change issue	Subject to change as needed
Non Functional requirements	Resources, reliability, integrity etc	Localized and on demand, no integration
Testing	By IT for enterprise use and scale	By users feedback
Funding	Annual budget cycle and payback reqs	Non req, but may distract from users time

Traditional vs. Situational Applications Development

Power in the Cloud: Using Cloud Computing
to Build Information Systems at the Edge of Chaos
(www.powerinthecloud.com)

Situational Business Processes and Choreography

While Situational Apps can be used as easily as business users use spreadsheets, there is another key dimension: Situational Business Processes (SBPs). While a situational application might be designed to do a specific task or handle a specific activity for a unique situation, the *choreography* and management of end-to-end business processes that make up any given value delivery system goes one giant step further. And that's where Business Process Management as a Service (BPMaaS) comes in. In other words, Situational Apps are a great advancement in delivering software applications, while Situational Business Processes are a great step forward in delivering business processes that tap and coordinate the process fragments contained in applications, situational or not. And the governance inherent in the use of the BOP's BPM system brings management control to "software gone wild" possibilities with Situational Apps.

The business processes that were once tightly confined within a single, vertically integrated company are blown to bits by the Internet and now stretch across multiple companies. These days, over 20 companies make up a typical value chain. Reassembling the business process bits from multiple companies into a coherent infrastructure is the centerpiece of 21st century business architecture. Think value webs, not value chains. The result is a web of any-to-any connections that can drive supply chains, demand chains, and even the business processes that represent the core competencies of an enterprise.

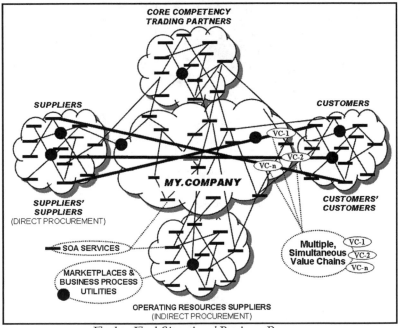

End-to-End Situational Business Processes

Companies must manage not just a single value chain, but multiple, individual value chains—simultaneously. The business processes that drive each value chain must be light weight and have the right level of granularity. That's where SOA comes in. With a SOA foundation, business process components can be bundled, unbundled and rebundled as "End-to-End Situational Business Processes" in response to new threats or opportunities. They can allow a company to participate in multiple marketplaces or reach out directly to individual customers with personalized offerings.

In the era of mass customization and personalization, a unique value chain may be needed for just a single customer and a single transaction (let's say VC-1). Others may serve multiple customers over long periods of time (let's say VC-2). Companies will need to manage both kinds of value chains and their underlying end-to-end processes for each *situation* (hence SBPs). Variations in sourcing, customer service support, products, and market channels will be unique to each value chain.

Just consider UPS. The company provides a world-class parcel delivery service, as we all know. But when the company got into the computer repair business, delivery was only a small part of the new value chain UPS would have to support. When a Toshiba laptop breaks down due to a hardware failure, UPS certified technicians in Kentucky do the repairs, requiring a whole new set of value chain resources and activities that must be managed.

The figure below depicts *hypothetical*, end-to-end, intercloud, situational business processes used to launch a killer new product.

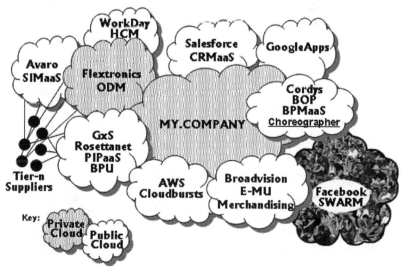

End-to-End Situational Business Processes

It's a hybrid Cloud mashup that's ready for a consumer swarm driven by Facebook and other social networks. Thought the iPhone was hot? Then the g-phone? Well, welcome to the sg-phone, the sun glasses phone that will obsolete all others. The heads-up display, ear pods and eye-wink cursor control, backed by voice commands, does it all. Conceived and patented by a scientist gone mad, Warren Buffet's Berkshire Hathaway immediately invested $2 billion on the condition that the product be brought to market in an instant. How'd you like to be the CIO that could make such possible?

Well, Claude Skydancer had a plan. On the design and production side, he would plug in the legendary original design manufacturer (ODM), Flextronics in Singapore, who in turn, would tap its suppliers using Avaro's Supplier Information Management as a Service (the same company GE uses) to source and manage any number of Tier-n component suppliers. Flextronics and its suppliers would also tap the GxS Rosettanet PIPaaS business process utility for B2B interactions, as well as Workday's human capital management (HCM) service for its 200,000 employees scattered over 30 countries.

On the customer-facing side of the endeavor, Salesforce.com was tapped for sales force automation, and Cordys' BOP served as the grand orchestrator, providing complete process life cycle control for the end-to-end business processes. As we'll elaborate below, because the trading partners operate on their own clocks, the BOP also serves as the "choreographer" of the entire value delivery system. Further the business process management system (BPMS) at the heart of the BOP provides real-time business intelligence (BI) and business activity monitoring (BAM) that's essential to continually optimize the overall value delivery system.

Google maps were mashed up to bring retailer locations into the picture. Finally, touching the swarm that would emerge at Facebook, Broadvision's E-MU merchandising system for mass customization was deployed. To get ready for the storm, Amazon's EC2 elastic compute cloud was put on standby for when the product launch became overwhelmed by Facebook and other social computing media.

Because the typical value chain is composed of multiple companies, companies that run under their own internal control and against their own internal clocks, the notions of orchestration and choreography come front and center. While the Cloud literature is full of writings on mashup applications the real challenge for the enterprise is orchestrating and choreographing "services" into end-to-end business processes that deliver value to the customer. That's where business process management delivered via a Business Operations Platform (BOP) in the Cloud comes in.

A BOP must incorporate both orchestration and choreography. With orchestration, there is a centralized control mechanism that directs activities, each of which is an interaction between services. While orchestration is how one *executes* a composition of services, it isn't the method by which one composes services. Choreography has no centralized control. Control is instead shared between multi-company participants in a peer-to-peer model. Choreography is at a higher level and looks at a process as message-passing between peers, without delving into the processes internal to any of the participants.

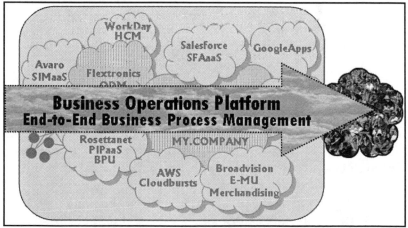

Business Process Choreography in the Cloud

Dr. Charlton Barreto of Adobe Systems said his favorite analogy for orchestration and choreography is Steve Ross-Talbot's analogy of a conductor of an orchestra (a director of a musical performance) representing Orchestration; and composition of dance into choreography by one or more participants (each dancer performs independently of central control, but in collaboration with other participants) representing Choreography. Particularly insightful in this analogy is the role of improvisation in Choreography, which is enabled by the neutral, peer-to-peer perspective. [1]

The technical discussions go deeper than we'll entertain here, but the business operations platform must include both orchestration and choreography due to the multi-company composition of today's value delivery systems.

The bottom line is that business process management (BPM) is the foundation for going beyond "mashup apps" and on to "mashup business processes." Companies don't want more software applications, they want business processes that deliver value to their customers, and such business processes are no longer "owned" by a single company, no matter how dominant that company is in the value chain.

As BPM pioneer Rashid Khan stated it, "With respect to mashups, I would strongly argue that BPM is one of the first application categories to offer mashups even before Web 2.0 was popularized. Think of the modern BPM 'client,' or the application that users use to participate in a business process and do their work. The BPM client is a classical example of a mashup. It pulls information from a number of sources such as databases, Web Services, EDMS (for document attachments), the BPM server (for status information), and often from integrations with other enterprise applications such as ERP and CRM. This information is collected in real-time and then presented to the user in a manner that is conducive to quick decision making and getting the job done. Of course, the ease and flexibility with which BPM applications allow these mashups to be created depends on the capabilities of the underlying BPM software that is used. However, the point is that the BPM client is a mashup that is used by all the participants in a process. Check one for BPM." [2]

From a business model perspective, our business becomes a "mediator" between supply and demand. We no longer are "sellers" to our customers, we become "buyers," going to the ends of the earth to bring the greatest value to our customers. Our customers become "prosumers" helping us to create maximum value across the entire value delivery system.

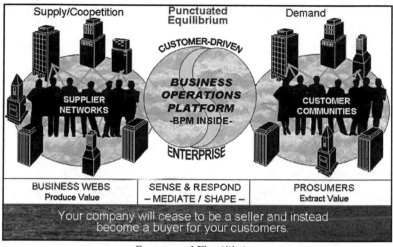

Punctuated Equilibrium

Yes, you can innovate, but your competitors soon catch up with you. So winning is a matter of "punctuated equilibrium" where you set "the pace of innovation." Innovate and disrupt. Then innovate and disrupt again … and again. In this new world, everything is customer driven, and customers are the only asset you have in the brave new world of total global competition.

So there you have it, choreography in the Cloud is the future of building customer-driven value delivery systems in 21st century businesses. Just a few years ago, value-chain dominance by an 800-pound gorilla orchestrating everything was the key to competitive advantage. Today it's process collaboration, cooperation, and choreography. Can your company teach elephants to dance?

In addition to handling operational requirements through process management, the Cloud will breed a new class of applications targeted at using technology to enable the automation of business leadership activities.

From Leadership to Business Results

Process veteran George Barlow of Cloud Harbor explains, "The business cycle relies on business leaders to create policies and strategies that are then executed through the processes of the business to produce business results. The evolution of software development for businesses has resulted in technologies that can automate the execution portion of the business cycle (business process management), and provide many views of business results (business intelligence). What has yet to be automated on a large scale is the creation and maintenance of policies and strategies.

"The next wave of business software enablement will center around Strategic Business Modeling (SBM). SBM will provide automation for the planning and rules (strategy and policy) segment of the business cycle. Here we will see a convergence of business frameworks and best practices for industries and vertical marketplaces (MES/REPAC, ACORD, eTOM, etc.), horizontal supply and value chains (SCOR, VRM, etc.) and compliance frameworks (SOX, BASEL II, ITIL, etc.) as well as mission, vision, goals, objectives, risk mitigation and other common business elements come together as cloud computing applications spanning every segment of an enterprise and extending these Cloud ecosystems across vendor-enterprise-customer organizational boundaries [phew!]. The use of Master Data Models (MDM and data reference models from industry frameworks will result in many entirely new global commerce pathways in the Cloud. These Cloud applications will also allow remarkable new "scorecard" applications that will measure plan (SMB) against actual (BPM/BI) in real time not only across the enterprise but between cooperating value chain partners as well."

Process on Demand
– Fantasy or Fast Track to Agility?

As we've discussed, without business processes the Cloud remains a passive environment. However, we need to be very clear; process management in the Cloud is not just about BPM Suites on demand. The term "BPM on Demand" is beginning to take on a new meaning when used in conjunction with cloud computing.

The traditional use of BPM on Demand is often used to describe Software as a Service that delivers a BPM Suite as a Service (BPMSaaS) much like customer relationship management (CRM) applications are delivered as a service (e.g., Salesforce.com). Both use a pay-per-use or subscription pricing model. BPMSaaS provides a full suite of BPM lifecycle capabilities, from modeling to deployment, and on to analysis and optimization. It's a third-party Cloud alternative to deploying a BPM Suite in house. But there is much more to BPM on Demand.

If we take the stance that the Cloud can deliver an infinite number of business software Services, then we need a mechanism that makes that easy to orchestrate and choreograph those Services. This is where "Process on Demand" comes in.

Process on Demand means having the capability to call up Services when needed to change or augment a process that is *already being executed.*

The Services we are talking about are not the usual, fine-grained ones normally associated with the IT world. These services are far more sophisticated than simple "get data/put data" activities. What we have are Services that contain:

- User Interface
- Business Rules
- Key Performance Indicators
- Meta data

In short, we have everything that makes a self-contained Service that can be incorporated into an end-to-end business process. Why do we need this type of capability?

In a word, simplicity

The concept of Process on Demand enables you to build dynamic processes that can be changed "on demand" to meet chang-ing business needs. This dynamic process selection provides a sub-stantial improvement in flexibility and reduces design complexity. But let's dig a little deeper to see if those advantages are sufficient enough to achieve the gains in agility, scalability, and robustness needed to meet the ever-changing requirements of today's business environment.

When developing business processes it is quite often very dif-ficult to determine what will ultimately be needed in terms of do-cumentation, sub-processes, timing and dependencies of tasks to accomplish some given requirement. For example, in designing a process to handle an insurance claim for a traffic accident, the ana-lyst may know that the customer will need to get his car assessed for repair and that a payment may or may not be forthcoming, but may not know the types of documentation (e.g., the mechanics costing, police witness reports, and hospital bills) that will poten-tially be required to process the claim, nor will he or she know the dynamics that determine which one or ones of possibly many doc-uments to use.

These interrelated paths through the claim process may al-ready have been defined by different people, in different parts of the organization as self-contained business Services or sub-processes, and may be changed frequently as the procedures and rules change. In such cases it is not possible for the main claim process to determine, even dynamically, what particular Services to use. All the developer knows is that a particular goal is to be achieved, but exactly which Services can be used to achieve it can-not be easily determined. Nor in fact does the developer really care—he or she simply wants the goal accomplished in an appro-priate way.

To solve this problem, we need a repository where we can keep the Services for use by the company. What differentiates these Services from sub-processes or data integration tools is that our Cloud applications know (via meta data) what each Service does, the circumstances in which it can be used, and the goals and outcomes that are required.

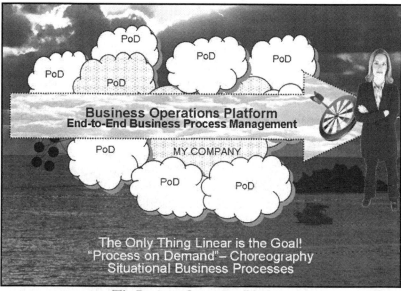

The Business Operations Platform

In addition, each Service is tagged with the circumstances in which it can be used, defined as an "entry condition" for the process. The entry condition is a conditional statement defined over the case data and any sub-process parameters. For example, the Service "Assess mechanical condition of vehicle" may be tagged with the entry condition "CarAge > 10" where CarAge is a field of the case data. Other services would be similarly tagged.

Such tagging allows us to define which required Services are available "on demand." By this means, the calling process simply needs to access a Service in the process flow, leaving it to the system to determine which business Service best achieves the goal in a given circumstance. During the execution of the process all those Services that satisfy the goal are known so that on evaluation of a value or the detection of an event, the Service that is required can be incorporated and executed in real time. This makes each iteration of the process totally different from previous or subsequent processes depending on the dynamics in play at the time.

Modern BPM capabilities allow us to use different Services for different goals and desired outcomes – all with no coding required.

The important point is that the condition that defines the "applicability" of the Service is attached to the Service, not the calling process. The calling process need not know or specify the selection criteria. This greatly simplifies the construction of the overall end-to-end process. The developer of the overall process need not know how many Services are available to achieve the desired outcome, their names, or the criteria that determines their use – all that needs to be known is that at least one such service exists.

The main process is simple, the "happy path," and is therefore easily understood. New services can be added or removed without any change whatsoever to the calling process or processes.

For example when an airplane lands at, let's say, London's Heathrow Airport, a sequence of events (a process) is triggered to quickly and safely prepare the plane for its next flight. The top-line process – prepare plane – is always the same, but the companies and individuals performing the parts of the overall process will change according to time of day, availability of components (e.g., jet fuel), next destination and myriad other reasons. The important thing is that the plane has everything done to it that needs doing – regardless of the Services used. The needed Services are changed dynamically depending on need.

However, how do we handle the exceptions, and less formal tasks of the case worker? What do we do when things don't go to plan or they can't be defined ahead of time ?

We all work in unpredictable business environments. So to understand how Process on Demand can help, we need to understand what people do. Knowledge workers have well defined objectives and goals but how they meet them depends on many factors – availability of documentation, response from others and so on. Therefore they have to keep track of their goals and their current situation, and then dynamically choose the sequence of tasks and processes that can meet their immediate needs. At each moment in time they select a sub-process that gets them from where they are to where they want to go next. And they continue to do this even as processes fail and unexpected events occur.

It should come as no surprise to learn that the same mechanism for handling exceptions and failures and the unexpected comes into play. For example, suppose a Service has been selected to achieve a given goal. If the Service fails or causes an error condition during execution, the calling process detects the event and swaps in a Service designed to handle errors. If a document arrives unsigned or filled in incorrectly, this can be noted and a different set of actions can be initiated to complete the task at hand. As a result, contemporary process management systems are far more robust for handling exceptions, failures, and incomplete process specifications.

Just as there may be many Services and methods for achieving a given goal, there also may be many internal and external providers of those Services. Process on Demand, using the loose coupling of Services, can make main processes easier to maintain, more robust and more elastic – reflecting the key benefits obtained from cloud computing as a whole.

However, the notion of Process on Demand as described here adds greatly to the robustness of Situational Applications. Conventional mashup application deployments tend to ignore the impact of possible failure of a service provider. What we have outlined is a well-grounded method for handling such situations. If a particular service provider cannot meet its agreed service level agreements, the on-demand nature of Process on Demand ensures that another provider will be contacted and brought into service. So if Company A cannot respond within the requisite timescales the application can turn its attention to company B and fulfill its needs from them without user intervention.

More complex applications can be built easier and faster simply because it is no longer necessary to encode all the special cases for dealing with a complex unpredictable world. In summary, the benefits of the Process on Demand approach are:

- Far quicker application development
- Faster ROI and time to value
- Applications that are easy to change and maintain
- Software that becomes more extensible and easily reused
- Software that is more robust and reliable
- Reduced complexity: simple, modular components, easily validated and inspected, self contained, accessible to both business

analysts and IT developers
- Development that can be done in bite sized chunks

Services as a Service

Forward-looking companies are turning their focus to the emerging field of Services Sciences, an interdisciplinary approach to the study, design, and implementation of services systems made up of people and technology to create and deliver value.

Irving Wladawsky-Berger, Chairman Emeritus of the IBM Academy of Technology, prefers to think of cloud computing as offering all kinds of *Services-as-a-Service* – consumer services, business services, government services, health-care services, educational services and so on. As advanced societies have transitioned from agricultural to manufacturing economies, the current transformation is to a service economy.

The services sector makes up 70 to 80% of GDP in advanced economies. The best way to define the services sector is to understand what it is *not*. It's not agriculture or manufacturing or construction, the *shrinking* sectors. In the U.S., agriculture accounts for only 1.4% of the gross domestic product and less than 2% of employment. Meanwhile, 4.3% of firms fall into the manufacturing sector, accounting for 12.5% of employment. In the UK, agriculture accounts for around 1.5% of employment, manufacturing for around 10%, and services for over 80%.

In short, up to about 75 % of wealth in industrialized countries is created *not* by growing food or making things, but by performing services: teaching, designing, delivering health care, banking, retailing, consulting, delivering IT services and so on.

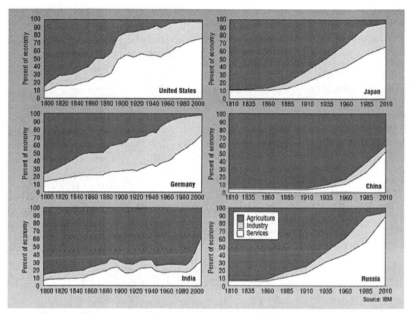

Services Represent a Growing Segment of the World's Economies

The link between science and agriculture and manufacturing is now a given and was ushered in over the last 200 years with the advent of the Industrial Age. But what about the link between science and services? The information technology to drive innovation in services have really only been around since the Web came on the scene in the mid-1990s.

IBM has been playing a leading role in this emerging field, which is no surprise for IBM had to transform itself as it looked over the abyss in the early 1990s. Lou Gerstner left RJR Nabisco to become IBM's CEO in 1993 and led the way to unlocking talent inside the once stodgy company. Hmm, a move from the "cookies and crackers company" to mighty Big Blue. What's up with that? *Services.*

Today, IBM pulls in the bulk of its revenues from services. Noting the lessons learned by IBM, HP bought EDS in 2008 and Dell bought Perot Systems in 2009. And last June, Howard Smith, coauthor of *Business Process Management: The Third Wave* was invited to speak at GE Global Research's *Whitney Symposium09* in Niskayuna, New York, a 600 acre research campus on the banks of the Mohawk river... the legacy of one Thomas Edison. It was an eye-opening experience (1,000 PhDs representing 22 disciplines in one campus). And you guessed it, the theme for the Symposium was *The Engineering of Customer Services.* GE gets it.

The keynote talk, *Business Process Management and Systems Thinking* was followed by Robert Morris, V.P. of Services Research and former director of IBM's legendary T. J. Watson Research Lab. Morris' talk was *The Transformation of IBM to a Technical Services Company.* To say the least it was an intense two days on the banks of the Mohawk.

Why, you might ask, were "BPM experts" at a *services* symposium? The following call-out from an IBM publication says it all in one sound bite:

> "Service science melds technology
> with an understanding of business processes."

While much activity in BPM centers on supply chains, logistics and other physical means of optimizing value delivery systems, that's not where the innovation action is in a service economy.

Yet, we have done little to take on services as the object of BPM initiatives as we don't really know much about what it takes to bring innovation to service processes.

As explained in the book, *Business Process Management: The Third Wave,* "A business process is the complete and dynamically coordinated set of *collaborative* and transactional activities that deliver value to customers." Well it's the *collaborative* part that is the challenge when it comes to services. Just consider the very nature of service processes:

- *Intangibility:* May be some combination of both intangible and tangible results or processes.
- *Heterogeneity:* Outcomes vary from one knowledge worker to another. Skills-based routing is vital.
- *Simultaneity:* Production and consumption occur at the same time. Complex Adaptive Systems: self-production, self-organization. Perceived control. Decision-making processes of

the customer.

- *Perishability:* May be consumed immediately. Can't be stored. Once the event or time has passed, the opportunity is gone forever.
- *Customization:* Services are almost always customized. Each transaction equates to a new "product."
- *Labor Intensive:* Products are capital intensive, services are labor intensive. People doing things for other people.
- *Resource Pull:* Appropriate service resources must be pulled on demand.

In physical supply chains customer demand is rarely perfectly stable, so companies do their best to make-to-forecast. Unfortunately, forecasts are rarely accurate and thus companies compensate by having a "safety stock." Going from the ultimate customer down to suppliers and suppliers' suppliers, each supply chain participant sees greater variation in forecast demand and thus has greater need for safety stock. In other words forecast variations are *amplified* as one moves downstream in the supply chain – the *bullwhip effect.*

While modern ICT technology can allow companies in a supply chain to move to a make-to-demand, versus make-to-forecast, model, how can the bullwhip effect be tamed when it comes to meeting the demand for immediate, perishable services? The *bullwhip effect* is even more accentuated in services industries where processes are less likely to be defined and a single service may require multiple unique processes.

What's the equivalent of safety stock in a services chain? Because safety stocks of knowledge workers cannot be stockpiled, that's where the emerging field of service science comes in to help answer questions of: "What types of technologies can come to bear on service processes?" Let's take a look at what's involved in the service value chain.

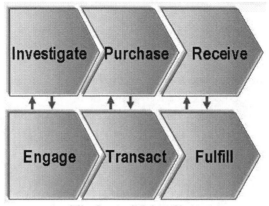

The Service Value Chain

A service process is a series of unique states involving the *co-production* of the provider and the consumer. Each "transaction" is a new product in itself, and the customer is a co-producer of the value rendered.

Too often, when we think of a service process, we think of what the provider must do, but such thinking results in frustration for the customer – who will defect in an instant. When we think of service processes, think of the customer as a co-producer of value. Think of migrating from transaction chains to information chains, and then on to knowledge chains (or peer-to-peer knowledge webs to be more precise). And, moreover, think about the Cloud and cloud computing technologies. The automation of business processes is a key enabler of the Cloud phenomena.

> Without process, the Cloud remains a passive environment that undoubtedly saves you money and removes some of the operational headaches, but does little else. The Cloud without process cannot deliver on the promise of services innovation.

All of the thoughts and ideas around quickly assembling Cloud-centered applications to support business services simply won't happen without process technology. As we explain later in this book, "Process on Demand" means having the capability to call up Services when needed to change or augment a process that is *already being executed*. This capability is an intrinsic part of the Service-Oriented Enterprise.

By taking service process management into the Cloud, services from multiple knowledge sources can be delivered with maximum flexibility and adaptability to meet the requirement that "most services must be customized." On-demand service processes aren't sequenced as in many traditional workflow systems. In contrast they are asynchronous and peer-to-peer, with the high-level process providing the choreography.

Let's turn our attention to the very core issues of providing services. When it comes to service forms of business processes, they reside in the domain of human-to-human interactions. Remember what was cited earlier, "People doing things for other people."

That is to say, services processes cannot be predefined or "flowcharted" in advance. In short, such collaborative human processes are "organic." They represent "emergent processes" that change not only their state, but also their structure as they are born, and then grow and evolve.

Such processes deal with case management and each service renders a unique process instance centered on human-to-human interactions. Keith Swensen writes in the book, *Mastering the Unpredictable* (www.mkpress.com/acm), "The facilitation of knowledge work or what is increasingly known as 'Adaptive Case Management' represents the next imperative in office automation. The desire to fully support knowledge workers within the workplace is not new. What's new is that recent advances in information technology now make the management of unpredictable circumstances a practical reality."

Case management in no way involves the kind of processes you call in IT to analyze, model and code – and get back to you in 18 months with a solution. As Keith Harrison-Broninski writes in his book, *Human Interactions* (www.mkpress.com/hi), "Human interaction management systems are peer-to-peer, choreographed processes, the kind needed to provide services that delight."

> "Processes don't do work, people do."
> -- John Seely Brown, Former Chief Scientist, Xerox

There's even more when it comes to services processes, something called Social Computing. Instead of hiring or outsourcing armies of call-center employees to meet peak demand, how about employing your customers as experts as described earlier in this book with the example of Intuit? In conclusion, it's not your father's BPM when it comes to service processes. Is your enterprise ready for the leap from BPM as we know it to Service Process Management (SPM) in the Cloud?

Takeaway

The advent of the Cloud means that the focus has moved up from technical infrastructure implementations to mechanisms that access and manage business Services as complete end-to-end business processes. This means that the ultimate measure of success is how the Services are consumed and whether that leads to new business opportunities.

One thing is certain in the world of unexpected change we now live in: More change, faster. The Cloud can help businesses become more responsive to change, of that there is no doubt. But at its heart lies the process layer, and that is where the Business Operations Platform can revolutionize the way business Services are delivered. The Cloud will be a huge collection of Services based on standards. Many Services can be integrated into existing business processes on the fly via Process on Demand capabilities, allowing organizations to become more modular and flexible—this is the stuff of competitive advantage in the 21st century.

References.

---

[1] http://charltonb.typepad.com/weblog/2007/05/what_is_choreog.html

[2] http://tinyurl.com/lsmkae

7. Enterprise Cloud Computing: The Process

Revolutions never go backward.
—Wendell Philips, American abolitionist.

It is not necessary to change. Survival is not mandatory.
—W. Edwards Deming

Key Points: The Successful Adoption Process

Having glimpsed at the trends and technologies of the Cloud as a new computing platform, and even more important, as a new business platform, the issues that come to top of mind are how to go about assessing the possibilities, undertaking due diligence, and capitalizing on the new business models—without getting burned. Businesses couldn't care less about just another gee-whiz technology, they want business results, they want business innovation. And so once a business sets its sights on cloud computing for competitive advantage, the fundamental question that follows is: "How do we get there from here?"

This chapter provides an overview of the strategic processes needed to adopt, deploy and successfully manage the Cloud as a business platform. This capstone chapter provides focus for many other topics in the book while emphasizing a business approach that leverages an organization's current information assets and development methods.

The success factors discussed in the chapter are based on a combination of theory and practical experience. After exploring the success factors, the chapter describes a systematic adoption *process* that incorporates those factors.

Funding Models at the Heart of Weathering Current Economic Conditions

As with all surveys, the questions inevitably influence the outcome somewhat. For example, if you ask a CIO if costs are important then you'll struggle to find one that says "no."

In 2009, an open-ended survey was conducted that focused on how CIOs felt in the current economic circumstances, and what role IT was playing in their organizations. This led quite naturally into a conversation about how well the IT role was being played. Should, or could, IT be playing other roles? And perhaps most crucially of all, the survey led to a comparison between how IT was used and how well their organizations were weathering unexpected change in the global economy. The results showed three common profiles of the CIOs surveyed:

- *Technology Utility* (24%) =
  IT is managed as a pure utility
- *Service Center* (39%) =
  IT assets are packaged to provide specific services
- *Business Technology* (37%)   =
  IT is a key asset in the leadership of the business

What lies behind these headline summaries is really interesting as 490 CIOs effectively ended up comparing notes on what, and how, things are working, or not working. The encouraging part is that a third of the CIOs now think the credit crunch has driven a reappraisal of how technology can genuinely move to be a revenue, margin, or performance enhancing part of the business model.

But can this really happen without attention to the funding model? IT has traditionally been a back office tool designed to centralize and improve key business processes and as a result, improve enterprise efficiency while reducing costs. As such IT has been treated as a "business cost" funded through the annual budgeting cycle as an overhead to be recovered. There are various ways to apportion this overhead, but at the end of the day it is a cost to the business, and like all other overhead, needs to be hammered down.

The pillars of an IT investment have been to invest a relatively large sum of money in a long project cycle, and then wait for a payback by gambling on the stability of the situation. At the end of a given IT investment cycle an enterprise *should* have a permanent competitive advantage.

The end result of this approach is that the ongoing costs of IT have increased so much that the headroom in the budget for new investment continues to decrease. When funding is in short supply and stability non-existent, the traditional pillars for starting new IT projects are not generally acceptable.

So CIOs should stop fooling themselves. In reality, much of the IT estate is a requirement to stay in business, is pretty stable in terms of the rate of change, is a genuine overhead, and should be treated as such in terms of ruthless cost management. To this end, data center consolidation by way of private Clouds is an option being deployed by many forward-thinking enterprises.

On the other hand, the value from using new technology that over a third of CIOs are aspiring to is focused on individual parts of the business in doing what they do uniquely, but doing it far better. That's not part of an enterprise-wide cost recovery overhead model of funding. It's a directly attributable cost to a specific business activity—and that's where the elasticity of the cloud computing model kicks in.

The pressure for new projects comes from two directions. One is from the cost-cutting CFO. The other is from specific functions directly related to the need for intelligence, decision support, and building new online products and services to sell. One of the key advantages of cloud computing is not just that we can build and deploy new business applications rapidly and at low cost, it's that we can implement new revenue-generating business models by using situational business processes in the Cloud as discussed in previous chapters. The challenge for the CIO is to make sure that this happens in a coherent and cohesive manner in the context of the entire enterprise.

Taking on such a role with a direct hand in supporting innovative business models is the challenge that a third of the surveyed CIOs are currently grappling with. Interestingly, these CIOs are working in the most successful enterprises.

In business life today, employees and those external parties who do business with our enterprises are evaluating and using technology as a key part of their work, and their business units' successes. In response to such changes it's time to consider how to adapt the funding model of the last century to one more suitable for the coming decades, especially in light of unpredictable change in the global economy.

Maryfran Johnson, Editor in Chief of *CIO Magazine* further sets the context for the challenge, "Cloud computing seems to have moved from an over-hyped industry buzzword to a serious topic worthy of attention for many enterprise CIOs. There are still big unanswered questions hovering around security and integration issues with cloud computing. But the global economic recession is clearly accelerating CIO interest levels in alternative ways to deliver software and services to organizations that are demanding ever-lower IT expenses while clamoring for ever-higher levels of computing support for collaboration and customer service."

It's in these contexts that organizations need to make thorough assessments and then plan their strategies for adopting cloud computing—or not.

Your Enterprise is What it Communicates

If you are a long-serving computing practitioner who has been through mainframes in data centers to mini computers in business units and then to PC networks everywhere, you might just recall hearing about Conway's Law. Well it's coming back again as we move into the Cloud. Melvin Conway's thesis first surfaced in 1968. Essentially Conway's point was that in designing business models the new model will mimic the enterprise's existing communication structure.

Conway's Law. Any organization that designs a system (defined more broadly here than just information systems) will inevitably produce a design whose structure is a copy of the organization's communication structure.

To understand the interest and why it comes up at times when technology innovation leads to business change, let's reflect on what it meant at the time of networked PCs, then what it means now in the context of the Cloud.

Each of our technology eras has resulted in a new business model, organizational structure, set of working methods, and perhaps most important of all, a new competitive value proposition. Okay that's not a new point, but at each shift there has been a key dependency on a core piece of technology which at the time seemed impossible to justify within the existing communication and organizational model.

Can you imagine working without email? Well in the early 90s most enterprises couldn't figure out the business case for email.

At the time the organizational model was both hierarchal and rigidly separated by departments, each of which had a departmental computer and set of applications that enabled the department to automate and keep track of its own processes and data. Though some office automation products existed such as IBM's Personal Services and Digital Equipment Corporation's All-in-One, paper and the interoffice memo ruled. Then networked PCs and client-server technology capabilities led to new business models based around business process reengineering (BPR) concentrating on optimizing the horizontal flow across the departments. On the people side, this introduced matrix work centered on a person's ability to perform his or her unique role in multiple cross-departmental processes. That's when the fun started.

Who was responsible to whom and for what? If the people still worked in departmental silos and the critical issue lay in a flow process in which their department performed a minor role, how did the issue get communicated? Did the issue have to go up the hierarchy within the department until a department head spoke to another department head?

Sounds silly now, but that's how it was at first. The whole point about email was that it changed *who could communicate with whom and about what* into a new communications structure that enabled the flexibility of matrix work within business processes rather than departments. In matrix work, email allowed communications among named people with clearly defined BPR roles. As we move toward the event-driven edge, every event is different and we don't know who has the relevant expertise. Therefore we get a flood of emails circulating to find anyone who might help. In contrast, social networks allow people to find each other on the basis of the issues and expertise and are thus very effective for the new collaborative ways of working enabled by the Cloud.

So how do we now shift toward a "services" model based on cloud computing with the focus on the optimization of events by deploying people's expertise if we are still working with the structure of matrix work? Who pays (time and money) for this collaborative stuff? It's the email issue of the 1990s all over again. Back in the '90s email arrived in the enterprise as increasing numbers of groups of workers started using different email products to be able to do the work that was now expected of them. So the fundamental driving force of optimization of the enterprise ended up being held back through the fragmentation of the communications structure. It's the same today.

Everywhere across the enterprise people with the most relevant expertise that can really make a difference are organizing collaboration tools for their own groups. At the top, denial of the need, or the fact that this is happening at all, is too often the order of the day. Hence, Conway's law is back again. It's there to help us to understand the link between communications and organizational structures when discussing how to change our business models.

Returning to Chapter 3 and Jeremy Rifkin's *Third Industrial Revolution*, the impact of communications on structure starts with society itself. So keep in mind that as society goes, so goes business and commerce. According to Rifkin, "The pivotal turning points in human consciousness occur when new energy regimes converge with new communications revolutions, creating new economic eras. The new communications revolutions become the command and control mechanisms for structuring, organizing, and managing more complex civilizations that the new energy regimes make possible." Thus the really big challenge of the Cloud isn't about technical issues; it's really about management and organizational issues.

Don't Climb Dangerous Mountains Without a Guide

Does the following scenario sound familiar? Your business faces mounting pressure to adapt to unexpected change in the economy. Customer expectations continue to climb, competitors are closing in. So plans are made to respond. These plans call for system capabilities that currently do not exist. You are in some part responsible for creating these capabilities within your organization. The tools at your disposal include current systems, infrastructure, staff and practices. Each of these represents a significant investment and currently provides value. But they are just not up to the task at hand. You know you need more, but more of what? There are numerous advanced technologies and techniques that could help, but which ones? And how do you implement them while leveraging your current investments?

In many ways the path to enterprise cloud computing is an obstacle course. Methods, tools and hype have proliferated to the point where it is very difficult for the busy professional to keep up, much less chart a safe course to the Cloud as a business platform.

In Switzerland, the famous Matterhorn casts a shadow over the town of Zermatt below. The cemetery at the foot of the mountain is a warning to those who would proceed up the steep slopes. Early pioneers who had neither maps nor guides are buried there, along with the primitive tools they thought were up to the task.

Today, Swiss law prohibits the inexperienced from climbing the steep slopes without a guide. Today's business and technology professionals tasked with adopting cloud computing should heed the message sent down from the Matterhorn: A guide is needed to survive the journey ahead. Because the trek is through territory unfamiliar to the inexperienced, even years of knowledge and skill in somewhat related domains do not directly apply. Too much is at stake to go it alone without an experienced guide to point out opportunities as well as pitfalls. The guide's map shows many alternative paths, and the guide charts the paths based on current circumstances and the goals of the climber.

But when it comes to cloud computing, that guide isn't necessarily just an experienced consulting firm, though it could very well be one of the new Cloud brokerage firms we discussed earlier in the book. Companies should also seek guidance from consortia and standards groups including The Open Group, the Cloud Security Alliance, the Cloud Computing Group, W3C, and the Object Management Group. Companies that want to win will participate and contribute to these groups, setting the stage for the future. We'll discuss this a little more in the assessment section below. See Appendix E for additional resources.

Characteristics of Successful Technology Adoption

Most organizations recognize the need to adopt new technologies to meet their business objectives. However, change must be carefully managed, and effective management calls for knowing which facets need to be monitored and controlled. Experience indicates that several factors are key to the successful adoption of cloud computing:

- Preserving and leveraging existing (legacy) systems
- Investing in service-oriented methods and business process management
- Transitioning staff to new skills
- Emphasizing architecture to facilitate system evolution
- Defining a process to apply new technologies

Legacy Systems Continue to Add Value

Clearly, current information systems do not fully meet the needs of today's rapidly changing and increasingly complex business environment. But they represent a significant investment and still provide value by supporting current business operations. Any new computing environment must leverage this investment in legacy systems. The schedule for any eventual retirement should be based on a balance of business and technical issues. The following process is based on experience and demonstrates tactics that can be used to leverage existing investments in legacy systems by including them in a cloud computing environment:

- Identify the logical content of the existing system in terms of the information and functionality it provides.
- Express the system contents as abstract interfaces that exclude implementation details: Service-Oriented Architecture (SOA).
- Appropriately publish these interfaces on a private or public Cloud.
- Direct new situational applications or situational business

processes to the new interfaces.

Today, many IT systems interact through interface files. Data is exported from one system and imported into another. Before long, these interfaces consume more resources than the systems they interconnect. But with the growth of cloud computing, the legacy system's contents are defined as abstract interfaces and published on public or private Clouds as "services." Publishing such services would create havoc unless they are governed by a Service-Oriented Architecture (SOA) to bring reliability, security and other necessary characteristics to the table. Clients (people or other systems) gain access to the system's data and functionality through this services interface. These clients are now insulated from the actual implementation of the system (abstraction) because they see it only as an abstract interface such as "Forecast, Order, Remit, Cancel, Supply and Receive."

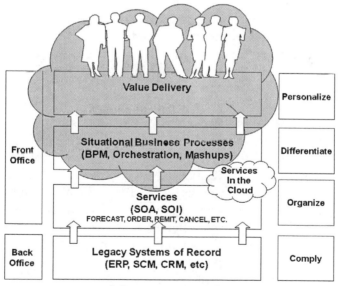

Migrating to the Cloud

Over time, legacy systems can be reengineered with whatever technology is appropriate. Because clients see the system as an abstract interface, they are unaffected by such change. This overall process is known as *wrapping* a legacy system so that business process fragments (e.g., Forecast, Remit, Supply and Receive) are exposed as standardized services. The near-term benefit of SOA is increased access to information and functionality. The long-term benefit is simpler and safer migration to cloud computing.

Exposing business process segments as services also provides an opportunity to publish a system's true *semantic contents*. Users typically extend a system through *usage patterns*. For example, multiple billing options may be required for customers of a manufacturing company. Even though the current system does not support this feature, a user may enter information about the same customer several times with various options. When an order is taken, the entry with the desired billing option is selected. As a result of this multiple entry, the total number of customers in the system does not reflect the real customer population. Users may also employ special codes or note field entries to extend a system beyond its original design.

Analyzing *extended usage patterns* is critical to understanding the actual information and functionality supported by existing systems. Extended usage patterns are not seen when studying the technical data and functional documentation of the legacy system. Exporting the contents of a system through an abstract services interface provides an opportunity to include these patterns of usage in the public definition of the system.

Filtering mechanisms and business rules must be inserted to match the usage patterns. In this way, knowledge usually retained in individuals' heads is distributed throughout the organization – and throughout the extended value chain which, via the Cloud, may consist of millions of users. For example, the services of airlines or banks can have unintended uses that will be repurposed and reused by thousands of companies that mash them up into unique business offerings rendered to social media such as Facebook. Governance and policy implications for such business services go far beyond the governance and policy issues contained in yesterday's enterprise systems. Furthermore, situational business processes, whose unintended contexts draw on a given company's core processes, will become the norm and they must be managed as diligently as all other mission-critical business processes.

Service-oriented infrastructures are now being used in mission-critical applications. The benefits are clear. Elements of the business are clearly visible in the software. The conceptual gap between technology and business is narrowed. In addition, "services" represent unified combinations of data and function that are independent of their context. This means that they may be used in multiple settings. Cloud computing puts resources where they are needed most. Business process management tools can be used to create systems from reusable services that more accurately reflect real world concepts.

As shown in the figure below, the functionality of the legacy system includes Forecast, Order and Cancel. However, as users of the system gain experience, they will extend usage of the system to include a special forecast for holidays (Holiday Forecast) and procedures to expedite orders (Expedite Order). They will also mashup services from multiple sources to build ever more unique business offerings for their customers.

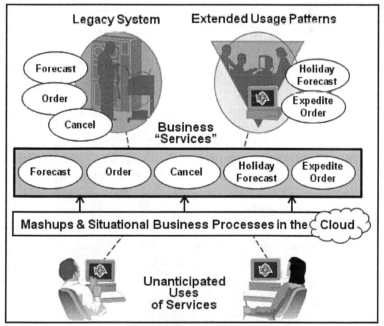

Extended Usage Patterns

Companies may turn to public Cloud services, such as Google Apps or Google maps, to "mashup" new functionality to enhance the end user experience. In addition to mashup applications, they may also develop situational business processes to meet the needs of unique customers, market segments or internal work groups. Regardless of the means used to extend a legacy system, capturing the functionality of both the original system and its extended usage is critical to publishing services.

Properly wrapping a legacy system to expose its services in a standardized fashion can extend its useful and economic life and minimize disruption when its implementation is reengineered. The benefits include a universal definition, increased availability and a pathway for evolution. A service-oriented infrastructure provides the basic building blocks for Cloud-oriented system development.

Traditional IT is based on using computers to push data in a fixed format to users, whereas Cloud services are about users being able to select and pull what they want to use in the context that suits them. This is the goal of exposing components of legacy systems as services. This is also why we speak of services as units of business, not units of technology. We're not interested in exposing programming interfaces for application integration; we're interested in exposing business services for business process integration.

Developers Apply New Skills to New Challenges

Accelerating change in the business environment has placed more and more demands on today's systems development professionals. The adoption of new technologies and techniques places yet more demands on developers as new methods and tools are applied to more complex problems. The only way to ensure successful adoption of cloud computing is to successfully transition information system developers. Current system development staffs embody significant value and intellectual capital. They understand the current systems and infrastructure. They also possess extensive domain knowledge that takes years to accumulate and that may not exist in written form. Cloud computing requires developers to:

- Adopt new *problem-solving* approaches

- Master the use of new *tools*
- Understand new *processes*
- Work in new extended *organizations*

Since the style of thinking that creates a problem cannot be used to solve it, new approaches to *problem solving* are needed. Although the term "paradigm shift" has become trite, the cliché does bear the truth that a fundamental shift in thinking is required to apply cloud computing effectively. For example, although developers may have experience using service-oriented architecture (SOA) for application integration, they may not have made the leap to applying SOA to business services (we discussed the many issues related to SOA in Chapter 5). Furthermoe, the classroom has not proven adequate for learning Cloud-generation computing. Participants won't learn to climb the Matterhorn while sitting in a classroom. Learning new ways of thinking and problem solving is best accomplished in the real world through mentoring and hands-on training. People need time to assimilate new concepts and reinforce them through experience with real business projects.

Examples of new *tools* include business process modeling and simulation tools in addition to technical tools needed for virtualization of computing infrastructure resources. Each tool extends a developer's capabilities, but also requires new skills. Time and experience are needed to develop competency and proficiency with cloud computing environments.

Enterprise-scale projects that apply cloud computing are often staffed by multiple development teams. These teams may be remotely located and have their work periodically integrated for testing. Attempting this scale of development without a well defined *process* is a sure recipe for failure. Not all developers are accustomed to operating under a well defined process. Practices like quality assurance may be resisted. Education will help developers see the value of a development process and training can provide the comfort level needed to be effective in cloud computing environments.

The adoption of cloud computing is more about roles and less about titles and reporting hierarchies. Many of the underlying technologies are better applied under an incremental process where teams work together to advance the development process. Team-based *organizations* may be new to some developers as well project support tools such as Human Interaction Management Systems (HIMS) needed for goal-oriented collaboration. Adopting new technologies places extensive demands on developers and their managers, even those fully accomplished in the world of Tradition-al IT. Both are expected to change the way they think and work as individuals and in groups. Learning should not be viewed as a one-time event. A learning organization is needed to promote conti-nuous learning. The key to a successful transition is setting clear goals and giving developers the time and opportunity to learn from their successes and mistakes. A key concept in this approach is the assessment of developers based on seven levels of mastery and subsequent curriculum creation to advance them through these levels (adapted from Meiler Page-Jones):

1. *Innocent:* Never heard of cloud computing.
2. *Aware:* Has read something about cloud computing.
3. *Apprentice:* Has studied cloud computing and knows just enough to be dangerous on his or her own.
4. *Practitioner:* Ready to use cloud computing methods and tech-niques on at least one significant project.
5. *Journeyman:* Uses underlying cloud computing technology natu-rally and doesn't require the assistance of a mentor.
6. *Master:* Has internalized cloud computing and knows when to break the surface rules. Beyond the "what's" and "how's," the Master knows the "whys" of cloud computing.
7. *Expert:* Writes books on and lectures about cloud computing, publishes learned articles, gives lectures and develops ways to push the envelope and extend methods and technologies.

In short, knowledge transfer is the key to success in imple-menting cloud computing. Tapping cloud computing as a business resource is not a big-bang conversion. The seed must be planted, initial cloud infrastructure services put in place, and pilot projects undertaken to establish the needed competencies. Having estab-lished such a greenhouse for nurturing competencies based on the seven-stage process of mastery, a company can grow into becoming a mighty, agile enterprise.

At some time during the journey from Innocent to Master, an epiphany will occur. It will be something like, "This is as it should always have been." However, no methodology and no technology is a silver bullet—including those associated with cloud computing. The ability to harness cloud computing for competitive advantage and business innovation will advance in step with the growing communal knowledge of those who master it. With collaboration and interaction being at the root of Web 2.0 and similar techniques, the way IT developers work needs to be realigned and attuned to Cloud-based platforms.

There's an old computer programming maxim that says, "To make things difficult when it comes to using computers is easy. To make things easy is difficult." This section has addressed the new skills needed by IT developers to created the ease-of-use required by business users who, in turn, will be able to create their own situational apps and business processes with relative ease. In sum, new information technology (IT) skills are needed for the IT staff to deliver business technology (BT) to their business communities.

Architectural Thinking Allows for Change

The velocity of change continues to increase. Accommodating change requires deliberate planning. Planning for change is one of the goals of software architecture. The reality is that all systems have an architecture. The real questions are how visible is the architecture and does it provide for business and technical evolution?

Keeping in mind that cloud computing isn't a new technology, organizations shouldn't think that their existing approaches to the development of Enterprise Architecture should be discarded. On the other hand, existing architectural frameworks will need to be adjusted to meet the unique challenges of cloud computing, most of which have to do with security and governance and the outside-in perspective needed for developing and consuming "services."

> Because technology is a fundamental part of an enterprise,
> a systematic method that keeps business requirements
> at the heart of any technology transition is absolutely essential.

Considering that cloud computing can be disruptive at many levels in the enterprise, Enterprise Architecture plays an increasingly vital role. An Enterprise Architecture describes business functions, business processes, people, organizations, business information, software applications and computer systems, tying their relationships to enterprise goals.

The Open Group is a vendor and technology neutral consortium whose vision of Boundaryless Information Flow™ will enable access to integrated information within and between enterprises based on open standards and global interoperability. The Open Group has been around for 25 years, claims over 7,800 participants from 350 member enterprises and works with other frameworks and standards organizations.

Building an Enterprise Architecture is a *process* and The Open Group Architectural Framework (TOGAF) is one of the most widely used reference architectures. At its heart is the Architectural Development Method cycle shown in the figure below.

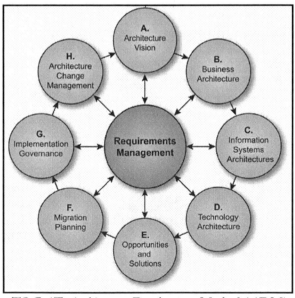

TOGAF Architecture Development Method (ADM)

The latest release, TOGAF 9, provides guidance on how to

use the framework to develop Security Architectures and Service-Oriented Architectures (SOAs). Two new standards include the Service Integration Maturity Model (OSIMM) and the SOA Governance Framework. OSIMM provides an industry recognized maturity model for advancing the adoption of SOA and cloud computing within and across businesses.

The SOA Governance Framework is a guide for organizations to apply proven governance standards that will accelerate service-oriented architecture success rates. The SOA governance framework may be used in the context of other governance frameworks, such as ITIL (Information Technology Infrastructure Library).[1]

TOGAF is known for the Architecture Development Method that is often used along with other frameworks like the Zachman Framework taxonomy to document contents. But with TOGAF 9 organizations can use the comprehensive Architecture Content Framework (ACF) Metamodel without other supplements.

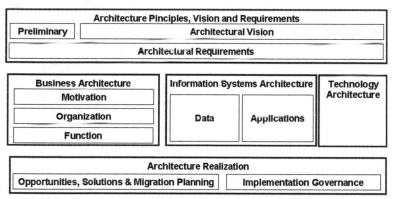

TOGAF Architecture Content Framework (ACF) Metamodel

While a solid architectural framework can provide guidance, organizations should be wary of cookie-cutter checklist approaches to adopting cloud computing. We avoid any such prescriptions in this book and in our professional work. We do however emphasize the special roles of Service-Oriented Architecture (SOA) and Process-Oriented Architecture (POA) for it is indeed the orchestration of services into end-to-end business processes that is the mark of *enterprise* cloud computing. While many architectural frameworks focus on computer applications, businesses don't want more computer applications; they want business process innovation for its business processes that deliver value to their customers. We amplify this emphasis in a section below and describe Cloud-Oriented Business Architecture (COBA) which fits naturally into the TOGAF framework.

Cookie-cutter checklists—No!
Cloud-Oriented Business Architecture—Yes!

Cloud platform technologies increase developer productivity through new tools and techniques. But creating applications is just the beginning. Cloud-based systems are expected to evolve throughout their lifetime, and that's where business process management comes in to govern the complete process lifecycle.

> The ability to *change*
> is now more important than the ability to create
> and that's where business process management comes in.

In the way that distributed computing architectures changed the world of IT by providing standard components, Cloud-Oriented Business Architecture (COBA) opens new possibilities for organizations to do the same at a *business* rather than the IT level. COBA represents the fusion of SOA and business process management Process-Oriented Architecture (POA), set in the context of cloud computing infrastructures and platforms. When we speak of SOA or POA we are also talking about "units of business" versus "units of technology." (See Martyn Ould's book, *Business Process Management, A Rigorous Approach*).

In short, COBA = (SOA + POA) x Cloud Infrastructures

COBA, centered on "Situational Business Processes (SBPs), will open new frontiers in how enterprises redesign their value chains to deliver their goods and services. Sound complicated? Business is complicated, and it's now completely driven by customers who expect what they want, when and where they want it. Call it mass customization. Call it the new reality of 21st century business.

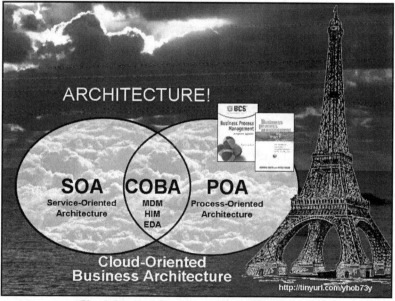

Cloud-Oriented Business Architecture (COBA)

As companies adopt SOA to provide standardized services, IT's contribution to the business grows exponentially. In the world of SOA, services are business process fragments that can be reused in many contexts and settings. Those reusable process fragments can be tapped as companies design end-to-end SBPs to support multiple value chains. That is, SBPs can be adapted to new projects, new initiatives, new campaigns and new lines of business.

The key to making this possible is to free scarce IT staff from having to translate process designs into software code. With modern BPM tools, processes become first-class citizens and business processes are placed center stage in the world of developing new information systems. Using business process modeling tools, services can be incorporated into process models that can be deployed without typical program coding.

> No matter how long or short-lived SBPs may be,
> their design, implementation and improvement
> must be given the same level of care and attention
> given to all enterprise business processes.

Software flexibility and reuse enable business process flexibility and reuse. That's the stuff of Cloud Oriented Business Architecture in the hyper-competitive markets of the 21st century. COBA gives businesses the flexibility they need to form new bonds with customers and suppliers in real-time.

Let's assume that all of the bases are covered. Legacy systems have been included in development plans; new Cloud infrastructure services have been integrated into the development environment; and developers have become members of interdisciplinary work teams. Maybe some training on architectural thinking, planning and notations has also been included.

But, what makes it all come together? Those who study physics learned long ago that things do not just "come together." Entropy is the universe's never-ending march toward disorder. Software projects are no exception. They do not just "come together." *Architecture as a process* brings the ingredients together by interlocking people, technology and organization as a business builds Cloud-oriented systems on its legacy foundation. A well-defined architectural process identifies how development work should be done. It also includes measures for determining whether things are going according to plan. A feedback mechanism monitors the current process, determines its effectiveness, and suggests areas for improvement. Continuous process improvement is the key to long-term success.

"There is nothing new under the sun but there are lots of old things we don't know."—Ambrose Bierce, *The Devil's Dictionary*, 1906. The first principles of architecture developed since the advent of object orientation in the late 1960s haven't gone away, they have been advanced to take advantage of evolving Internet protocols. Request and respond principles remain at the core of modern IT architectures.

In the initial stages, companies will likely stay behind their firewalls and implement private Clouds to consolidate data center resources – and more importantly gain mastery of outside-in architectures and methods. They will embrace new architectural styles that make it possible to adopt distributed governance for identity management, security, access control and privacy.

From there, companies will grow and mature so they can then fully embrace scale-out public Clouds and hybrid Interclouds. Startup companies, on the other hand will leapfrog legacy migration and embrace cloud computing from day one. Unencumbered by legacy, newcomers are positioned to unleash "creative destruction" in existing industries, and even create whole new industries with new business models just as Animoto.com and DimDim.com have done—and Amazon.com did a decade ago.

The earlier companies gain mastery of cloud computing architectures, the more they will be strategically positioned to win in the Cloud economy.

A Successful Technology Adoption Process

We have outlined the characteristics of successful technology adoption. These factors require careful attention during the transition to cloud computing. Now we outline how organizations can adopt cloud computing by maintaining a focus on the critical success factors. As shown in the figure below, typical transitions move through three high-level phases.

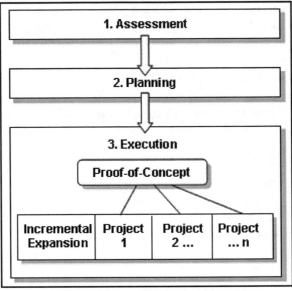

The Three Phases of Technology Transition

Assessment Defines the Destination

During an assessment, the experienced guide learns about the organization's goals and objectives. The guide (internal or external to the organization) documents the current capabilities of the systems, infrastructure and staff. An understanding of the current information systems development process is also acquired. This information is critical to ensure a successful transition and will be used in the planning phase.

Drawing from similar experience, the guide consults with the organization to describe possible alternatives to reaching its goals. Although several paths will be described and reviewed, the actual transition plan will reflect the specific needs and preferences of the organization. Regardless of the specific alternatives chosen, certain activities must be present to ensure success. Decisions must take into consideration available resources and sensitivity to risk. There is no "standard" transition plan since each business is unique.

Speaking of risks brings up the biggest fears of enterprises moving to cloud computing, number one being security. Security and privacy bubble to the top of concerns enterprises have when contemplating cloud computing. Just check out the IDC August 2008 244-member panel on cloud computing issues:

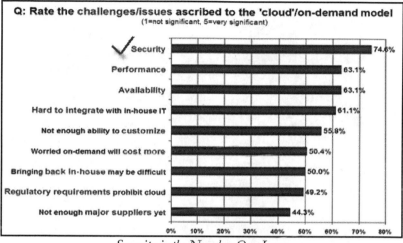

Q: Rate the challenges/issues ascribed to the 'cloud'/on-demand model
(1=not significant, 5=very significant)

✓ Security	74.6%
Performance	63.1%
Availability	63.1%
Hard to integrate with in-house IT	61.1%
Not enough ability to customize	55.8%
Worried on-demand will cost more	50.4%
Bringing back in-house may be difficult	50.0%
Regulatory requirements prohibit cloud	49.2%
Not enough major suppliers yet	44.3%

Security is the Number One Issue

Security is the number one fear of cloud computing. But there are also the wider concerns regarding the control and auditabilty of information systems whether they be located on premise or in the Cloud, or most likely a combination.

To begin, security in cloud computing, or *any* computing for that matter, is vital, although the requirements for security will vary widely depending on the application and data types. Some key issues include trust, multitenancy, encryption, and compliance. But Cloud security is a tractable problem; there are both advantages and challenges. Here are some of the advantages cited by NIST:

- Shifting public data to an external cloud reduces the exposure of the internal sensitive data
- Cloud homogeneity makes security auditing and testing simpler
- Clouds enable automated security management
- Redundancy and Disaster Recovery

The Many Issues Related to Cloud Computing

NIST cites some key security challenges:
- Trusting vendor's security model
- Customer inability to respond to audit findings
- Obtaining support for investigations
- Indirect administrator accountability
- Proprietary implementations can't be examined
- Loss of physical control

And NIST goes on to assert additional Cloud advantages:
- Data Fragmentation and Dispersal
- Dedicated Security Team
- Greater Investment in Security Infrastructure (far more than most individual companies can invest in)
- Fault Tolerance and Reliability
- Greater Resiliency
- Hypervisor Protection Against Network Attacks
- Possible Reduction of C&A Activities (Access to Pre-

Accredited Clouds)
- Simplification of Compliance Analysis
- Data Held by Unbiased Party (cloud vendor assertion)
- Low-Cost Disaster Recovery and Data Storage Solutions
- On-Demand Security Controls
- Real-Time Detection of System Tampering
- Rapid Re-Constitution of Services
- Advanced Honeynet Capabilities

But these additional advantages must be matched against the challenges of:
- Data dispersal and international privacy laws (In many cases privacy laws and other regulations require the cloud provider's resources to be in a particular location. The cloud provider and cloud consumer must work together to adhere to those regulations.)
  - EU Data Protection Directive and U.S. Safe Harbor program
  - Exposure of data to foreign government and data subpoenas
  - Data retention issues
- Need for isolation management
- Multitenancy
- Logging challenges
- Data ownership issues
- Quality of service guarantees
- Dependence on secure hypervisors
- Attraction to hackers (high value target)
- Security of virtual OS's in the cloud
- Possibility for massive outages
- Encryption needs for cloud computing
  - Encrypting access to the cloud resource control interface
  - Encrypting administrative access to OS instances
  - Encrypting access to applications
  - Encrypting application data at rest
- Public cloud vs. internal cloud security
- Lack of public SaaS version control

NIST further elaborates other Cloudy issues related to moving pri-

vate and sensitive data to the cloud:
- Privacy impact assessments
- Using SLAs to obtain cloud security
- Suggested requirements for cloud SLAs
- Issues with cloud forensics
- Contingency planning and disaster recovery for cloud implementations
- Handling compliance
  - FISMA
  - HIPAA
  - SOX
  - PCI
  - SAS 70 Audits

"We know that we cannot achieve absolute security unless we unplug the server, dump it in a big hole in a deserted location and forget about it."
—István Soós, Technology Consultant, Budapest, Hungary

While computer security has forever been a key business issue, what requires special attention is when information and processing go outside the "perimeters" of the organization. The Jericho Forum of The Open Group has developed its "Commandments" that must be observed when planning for a de-perimeterized future. See the Jericho Forum commandments in Appendix F.

If we take a technical view of some of the Cloud security issues, we can turn to a snippet from a Sun Microsystems white paper to see that "application architecture" is key, "Good security practices permeate every aspect of system design, implementation, and deployment. Applications must be secure by design, with interfaces that present only the appropriate data to authorized users. During implementation, developers must take care to avoid coding practices that could result in vulnerability to techniques such as buffer overflow or SQL injection. When deployed, operating systems should be hardened and every layer of software kept up to date with the most recent security patches. In cloud computing, applications are deployed in a shared network environment, and very straightforward security techniques such as VLANs and port filtering are used to segment and protect various layers of an application deployment architecture as well as isolating customers from each other. Some approaches to network security include:

- Use security domains to group virtual machines together, and then control access to the domain through the Cloud provider's port filtering capabilities. For example, create a security domain for front-end Web servers, open only the HTTP or HTTPS ports to the outside world, and filter traffic from the Web server security domain to the one containing back-end databases.

- Control traffic using the cloud provider's port-based filtering, or utilize more stateful packet filtering by interposing content switches or firewall appliances where appropriate. For even more fine-grained control over traffic, the concept of Immutable Service Containers (ISCs) allow multiple layers of software to be deployed in a single virtual machine, with pre-plumbed networking that is kept internal to the virtual machine."

As this book is not a technical treatise on security, let's move on to consider other issues. For implementers, we can recommend the book, *Cloud Security and Privacy* for a detailed treatment—in addition to the Jericho Forum commandments and the Cloud Security Alliance's "Security Guidance" (cloudsecurityalliance.org).

Of course there are many more issues to consider besides security, some presenting advantages, others disadvantages and others both advantages and disadvantages.

Radical reductions in traditional data center costs are high on the advantages list. Data centers are capital and labor intensive, and private clouds, whether hosted on premise or by a Cloud services provider, can dramatically reduce costs in many cases. Most of those hardworking smart folks working in today's data centers aren't spending most of their time building competitive new applications, they're dealing with maintenance and support nightmares. And then consider the headaches that go away when applications are capable of self-provisioning and maintenance and security issues are transferred to the Cloud service provider. Then, just maybe, in-house IT staff could spend a lot more time on building competitive advantage for their companies, and assisting business units in developing and improving their own business processes with highly-simplified Web 2.0-style Business Technology.

Cloud Security and Privacy

No, we are not at the end of the story of addressing cloud computing concerns, we are at the beginning. Enterprises should closely track, and participate in the work of several groups pursuing the standards needed for safe, secure, interoperable, cloud computing. But there's a problem for *there are so many standards to choose from.* To address this overchoice problem, in 2009, a group of standards bodies and industry groups joined forces to collaborate on a strategy behind future cloud computing standardization efforts. "Rather than one-by-one agreements and developing hundreds of standards that overlap, we're working together," Richard Soley, chairman of and CEO of the Object Management Group said during a panel discussion at the National Defense University Information Resources Management College's Cloud Computing Symposium.

The group of standards bodies, called "the Cloud Standards Coordination Working Group," includes the Distributed Management Task Force (DMTF), the Open Grid Forum (OGF), the Storage Networking Industry Association (SNIA), the Open Cloud Consortium (OCC) and the Cloud Security Alliance (CSA). Visit www.cloud-standards.org.

The body is looking at standardization in a number of specific areas, including security, interfaces to infrastructure-as-a-service, information about deployment such as resource and component descriptions, management frameworks, data exchange formats, cloud taxonomies and reference models.

The form and scope of those standards is to be determined, and Soley said the groups are looking for much more input from both users and industry. "Standards don't work without heavy participation by prospective end users of those standards," he said. To help facilitate that process, the bodies have set up a wiki to allow community and customer participation in determining the best paths for standards development.

"Community participation, deliberate action, and planning must be a vital part of any successful standards process," Gartner V.P. David Cearley said during a panel conversation. "Otherwise, cloud standards efforts could fail miserably. Standards represent those things that could absolutely strangle and kill everything we want to do in cloud computing if we do it wrong. We need to make sure that as we approach standards, we're approaching standards more as they were approached in the broader Internet—just in time."

Cearley brings up an interesting point. These very same issues were brought up as the Internet emerged on the business scene, and many companies shied away from the free-for-all, insecure, non-standardized Internet—until they got *Amazon'ed.*

> So it is that perhaps the biggest risk to a business
> is to look at all the risks, fear, uncertainty and doubt
> —and do nothing.
> When it comes to the assessment stage,
> focusing on cost, risk and other due diligence issues
> can belie the fundamental issue
> that the Cloud is really about a
> business platform for on-demand business innovation.

Focusing on on-demand business innovation doesn't mean tossing out due diligence, but it does mean that it's not the supply side of cost savings that will drive enterprise cloud computing, it's the revenue-generating demand side.

On the demand side, markets and individuals in those markets will *pull* and extract the greatest possible value from companies. They will use Social Networks to gain even greater control, for the power in economics will continue to shift from the producer to the consumer as never before.

Thus a company must establish a two-way, open dialog with customers, even though the customers' dialog may not always be favorable. If your company doesn't establish such dialog, your customers will go elsewhere to talk about you—there's no stopping it.

Bring customers into your product design processes as Dell does with Ideastorm.com.

Conduct "innovations jams" as IBM does with its Second Life avatars and thousands of employees and customers.

Got Facebook?

Planning Defines the Route

Once the assessment is complete, a plan can be built to realize the organization's goals and objectives. This plan includes activities that address the key elements of success.

Legacy systems are examined, and tasks are created to define their interfaces and integrate them into the service-oriented infrastructure. An infrastructure sub-plan addresses the selection, provisioning and integration of any required hardware, software, networking components or development tools whether provided in-house or by a Cloud service provider. Based on current developer skills, specific tasks are created for education and training. These factors require careful attention during the transition to cloud computing, and overall governance of business unit use of free or low-cost Cloud services needs specific attention.

Systems created under a well-defined architecture will exhibit the qualities of conceptual integrity. In the short term, this quality helps organize and manage the development process. In the long term, it facilitates business and technical evolution as well as corporate governance. The overall shape of the plan is governed by a process framework.

> Cloud-oriented development plans should be based on an architecture that allows for *change*.

During planning, tasks that will be executed in the near term are defined in detail. Long-term tasks are more generally scoped, abstractly defined and roughly estimated at this stage of planning. A mechanism must be provided to replace general or abstract tasks with more detailed versions as the project progresses and more is learned.

A major source of change is the business itself. The detailed initial plans are based on current business goals and objectives. On the other hand, adopting cloud computing is a long-term commitment. It's reasonable to assume that business conditions will change over time. Thus flexible plans require a service-based framework that permits changes to be made during any given project's execution.

Execution

Careful assessment and planning are essential to successful Cloud technology adoption. However, initial projects introduce change in virtually all facets of development:

- New development paradigm
- New infrastructure and developer skills
- New roles, responsibilities and organization

Because this much change all at once is a sure formula for unacceptable risks, proof-of-concept projects are needed.

A Proof-of-Concept Project Manages Risk

Fortunately, risk management can be achieved through proof-of-concept projects that introduce new facets in a controlled environment. A proof-of-concept project is planned in the same way as any other project. The differences lie in:

- Goal selection
- Project scope and duration
- Development pace

The goal of a proof-of-concept project is to balance risk and validation. The project must demonstrate value to the organization without introducing unnecessary risk. An organization does not want to bet the business, but the resulting Cloud-oriented application should not be a toy.

Look for low-hanging-fruit opportunities that have low risk, but where results can be highly visible. No-brainers include cloud-bursting to provide resources for peak demand (IaaS) and developing and testing new applications in a Cloud environment (PaaS), forgoing the need to install new hardware or software in-house.

Other opportunities include non-differentiating commodity applications (SaaS) and productivity tools such as email and Desktop as a Service (DaaS). Recall that GE replaced 400,000 seats of desktop productivity tools with Zoho, and the city of Washington D.C. did the same for 38,000 users with Google. Panasonic migrated 150,000 workers to IBM's LotusLive.

Cost-saving projects are good candidates for a proof-of-concept endeavor, but customer-facing, revenue-generating projects will be needed to go beyond the cost savings proposition of cloud computing and onto actually doing business and achieving business innovation in the Cloud. That's where BPMaaS comes in as the path to developing end-to-end business processes that deliver new value to your customers.

Business innovation vs. cost-savings considerations are especially important when going to Level 4 (BPM as a Service) where highly differentiating business processes are selected for development and implementation. These are the highest payback uses of cloud computing, and an enterprise need not climb the ladder from levels 1-3 before addressing business process innovation as the place to start in migrating to cloud computing. It may seem riskier, but when you consider that business process innovation is the key to competitive advantage, it's here that the true value of cloud computing is made visible with tangible business results.

By selecting a Cloud Service Provider that offers BPMaaS, the details and headaches of the lower tiers are left to the CSP. But choose your BPMaaS provider carefully for this is the unchartered territory of cloud computing and amateurs aren't welcome.

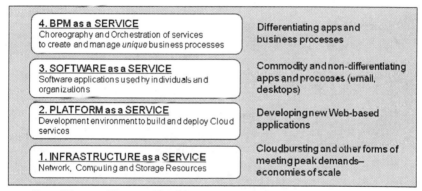

Low-Hanging Fruit at Each Layer of the Cloud Computing Model

Customer-facing pilots may be as straight forward as providing new value by delivering seamless access to information that was previously disjointed. This exercises the new infrastructure and provides improved decision-making. Since information remains available in its original form, no new business risk is introduced.

The scope and duration of a proof-of-concept project is usually limited to a maximum of 30 days. In his book, *The Greatest Innovation Since the Assembly Line*, award winning CIO, Michael Hugos describes such a project as the "30-Day Blitz." If more time is needed, as this is indeed a first proof-of-concept project, so be it.

The short duration and limited scope brings the project to closure so that the effectiveness of the new technology can be assessed.

Required adjustments can be made before moving on to additional projects. In many cases, the development pace for a proof-of-concept project is generally slowed to allow developers time to learn. Tasks are structured to provide early opportunities for success. It is important that developers build confidence in themselves before moving on to more aggressive schedules. New concepts require hands-on experience and time to be assimilated.

Beyond new custom development projects, pilots will include experimenting with social media, keeping in mind corporate governance. There's a lot to experiment with and lots to learn. Here are some examples of social media software applications:

Communication:
- Blogs: Blogger, LiveJournal, Open Diary, TypePad, Word-Press, Vox, ExpressionEngine, Xanga
- Micro-blogging and Presence applications: Twitter, Plurk, Jaiku
- Social networking: Bebo, Facebook, LinkedIn, MySpace, Orkut, Skyrock, Hi5, Ning, Elgg, Google's Open Social
- Social network aggregation: NutshellMail, FriendFeed
- Events: Upcoming, Eventful, Meetup.com

Collaboration:
- Wikis: Wikipedia, PBwiki, wetpaint
- Human-to-Human Collaboration: Humanedj.com
- Social bookmarking (or social tagging): Delicious, Stumble-Upon, Google Reader, CiteULike
- Virtual worlds: Second Life, Forterra
- Social news: Digg, Mixx, Reddit, NowPublic
- Opinion sites: epinions, Yelp, Znopit

Multimedia:
- Photo sharing: Flickr, Zooomr, Photobucket, SmugMug
- Video sharing: YouTube, Vimeo, sevenload
- Livecasting: Ustream.tv, Justin.tv, Stickam
- Audio and Music Sharing: The Hype Machine, ccMixter

We could go on. Instead, do your own search for "social media" as new offerings emerge every day.

Incremental Delivery Sets A Sustainable Pace

Upon the completion of the proof-of-concept project, any needed adjustments will be made to the development infrastructure and supporting processes. In addition, governance policies that control the free-for-all use of readily available public cloud computing offerings are put into place. Otherwise government and corporate compliance issues will raise their ugly heads.

From this point forward, an incremental delivery philosophy should be adopted. Ideally deliverables should be made via the 30-day Blitz as business results are what counts and companies can no longer tolerate drawn-out 18-month IT development projects where systems are delivered just after their usefulness has ended. Of course once services and platforms are developed to support situational business applications and processes, deliverables can be immediate: from the 30-day Blitz to the 30-minute Situational Business Process.

Frequent deliveries allow the organization to change priorities and direction when appropriate. This arrangement also enhances credibility with customers and builds morale among developers and business stakeholders. From a quality perspective, each delivery provides useful feedback for continuous process improvement.

Takeaway

When properly applied, cloud computing can provide significant benefits to an organization. This chapter described the *critical success factors* for migrating to cloud computing and outlined an adoption *process* for applying these success factors. The process takes into account the investments in existing systems and Enterprise Architecture provides the methods to leverage these valuable assets.

The process builds on the foundation of legacy systems, and orchestrates the people, technology and organizations needed to adopt cloud computing for business advantage. Since the economic crisis of 2008, the magnitude of change is so great that it is forcing organizations to migrate to the Cloud. Although an organization can go it alone, an experienced guide can show the way and allow a company to maintain its business focus during the journey ahead.

References.

[1] The names ITIL and IT Infrastructure Library are registered trademarks of the United Kingdom's Office of Government Commerce (OGC).

8. Epilog

For the world has changed, and we must change with it.
—President Barack Obama, January 20, 2009

Make no small plans; they have no magic to stir men's souls.
—Spencer W. Kimball

This book has presented the fundamentals and the current state-of-the-art of enterprise-class cloud computing. Cloud computing no doubt has the potential to disrupt current enterprise IT practice and represents the next rEvolution in the history of business technology—indeed, the next rEvolution in business.

But there are many unanswered questions about cloud computing, especially related to security. So let's let Mather, Kumaraswamy and Latif address that issue from their book, *Cloud Security and Privacy*, "A great part of the concern today about cloud computing security and privacy is based on unfamiliarity—it's new, and not enough people understand it well enough to make informed judgments. Real security issues for and by Cloud Services Providers absolutely exist today. However, better understanding, greater transparency, and better security technology capabilities going forward mean that the hue and cry of today over the Cloud's lack of security will soon fade, and will become yesterday's concern."

Okay, check one off the list of concerns.

But now consider,

"There is a tide in the affairs of men,
Which, taken at the flood, leads on to fortune;
Omitted, all the voyage of their life
Is bound in shallows and in miseries."
—Julius Caesar Act 4, scene 3, 218–224

The rising tide we've highlighted in this book isn't about some gee-whiz new technology; it's the rising tide in the larger society in which businesses must operate. Let's return to social thinker and author, Jeremy Rifkin from Chapter 3, "The pivotal turning points in human consciousness occur when new energy regimes converge with new communications revolutions, creating new economic eras. The new communications revolutions become the command and control mechanisms for structuring, organizing, and managing more complex civilizations that the new energy regimes make possible. For example, in the early modern age, print communication became the means to organize and manage the technologies, organizations, and infrastructure of the coal, steam, and rail revolution. It would have been impossible to administer the first industrial revolution using script and codex. Each more sophisticated communication revolution brings together more diverse people in increasingly more expansive and varied social networks."

The important issues we've explored in this book are far more about the changes in the bigger society outside the world of business. If cloud computing were all about internal cost reduction, then Moore's law could possibly mean that cost savings in the data center was the real issue and that virtualization and new blade server systems would solve the problem of cost containment. Discussion finished.

But as we've explored, the world is changing.

Now, the only certainty is uncertainty itself.

And so it is that the ability to change is the central competency the enterprise must pursue. And the enterprise must pursue change with the recognition that technology and business are not only intertwined, they are fused as one. Furthermore, because social computing is changing the very fabric of society across the globe, the enterprise must keep in step with this systemic change.

A common thread throughout this book has been the subordination of technology issues to business issues when addressing cloud computing. We don't want to speed up what we already do, we want to transform our businesses to meet the realities of the current society and economy. We no longer look to technology for saving money or for defensive strategy. Cloud computing provides us with offensive, front office business tools that we can use to disrupt the status quo in our industries and to make money. But while you can sign up for Cloud services from a number of cloud service providers, you cannot buy a strategic business plan. So cloud computing isn't something you go out and buy; it's an enabler for executing on innovative business ideas. If you don't have such, don't bother.

In the same way that the computer heralded the end of the industrial age and the beginning of the information age, cloud computing heralds an age of *knowing* versus predetermined knowledge. Not only can cloud computing distribute an enterprise's existing knowledge, it can reach out to social networks to keep the enterprise "in the know." This capability empowers the individual, whether on the shop floor or in a customer's office, to make optimal business decisions on-the-spot, when and where required.

This is the magnitude of empowerment that is required for true business innovation. With such empowerment, something very new starts to happen. Enterprises begin to change the very ways they conduct business.

On the other hand, cloud computing isn't a crapshoot. If enterprises do not apply the tools and methods that underpin cloud computing within the context of a solid Enterprise Architecture, cloud computing will provide no value and create chaos. At the heart of Enterprise Architecture is Process-Oriented Architecture, for business process management gives business people direct control over their business processes by obliterating the business-IT gap.

To Cloud or not to Cloud?

That indeed is the question.

If you came to the pages of this book looking for a cookie-cutter solution for the changes we all face, then all we can say is, "Look elsewhere."

Only you can invent your future, and we hope we have set a context and provided a framework for you to do just that.

A. Cloud Computing Use Cases

This Appendix is adapted from the Cloud Computing Use Case Discussion Group.[1]

End User to Cloud

In this scenario, an end user is accessing data or applications in the cloud. Common applications of this type include email hosting and social networking sites. A user of Gmail, Facebook or LinkedIn accesses the application and their data through any browser on any device. The user doesn't want to keep up with anything more than a password; their data is stored and managed in the cloud.

Most importantly, the user has no idea how the underlying architecture works. If they can get to the Internet, they can get to their data.

Requirements

- **Identity**: The cloud service must authenticate the end user.
- An **open client**: Access to the cloud service should not require a particular platform or technology.
- **Security**: Security (including privacy) is a common requirement to all use cases, although the details of those requirements will vary widely from one use case to the next. A full discussion of security in cloud computing is beyond the scope of this paper.
- **SLAs**: Although service level agreements for end users will usually be much simpler than those for enterprises, cloud vendors must be clear about what guarantees of service they provide.

Enterprise to Cloud to End User

In this scenario, an enterprise is using the cloud to deliver data and services to the end user. When the end user interacts with the enterprise, the enterprise accesses the cloud to retrieve data and / or manipulate it, sending the results to the end user. The end user can be someone within the enterprise or an external customer.

Requirements

- **Identity**: The cloud service must authenticate the end user.
- An **open client**: Access to the cloud service should not require a particular platform or technology.
- **Federated identity**: In addition to the basic identity needed by an end user, an enterprise user is likely to have an identity with the enterprise. The ideal is that the enterprise user manages a single ID, with an infrastructure federating other identities that might be required by cloud services.
- **Location awareness**: Depending on the kind of data the enterprise is managing on the user's behalf, there might be legal restrictions on the location of the physical server where the data is stored. Although this violates the cloud computing ideal that the user should not have to know details of the physical infrastructure, this requirement is essential. Many applications cannot be moved to the cloud until cloud vendors provide an API for determining the location of the physical hardware that delivers the cloud service.
- **Metering and monitoring**: All cloud services must be metered and monitored for cost control, charge backs and provisioning.
- **Management and Governance**: Public cloud providers make it very easy to open an account and begin using cloud services; that ease of use creates the risk that individuals in an enterprise will use cloud services on their own initiative. Management of VMs and of cloud services such as storage, databases and message queues is needed to track what services are used.

  Governance is crucial to ensure that policies and government regulations are followed wherever cloud computing is used. Other governance requirements will be industry- and geography-specific.
- **Security**: Any use case involving an enterprise will have more

sophisticated security requirements than one involving a single end user. Similarly, the more advanced enterprise use cases to follow will have equally more advanced security requirements.

- A **Common File Format for VMs**: A VM created for one cloud vendor's platform should be portable to another vendor's platform.

- **Common APIs for Cloud Storage and Middleware**: The enterprise use cases require common APIs for access to cloud storage services, cloud databases, and other cloud middleware services such as message queues. Writing custom code that works only for a particular vendor's cloud service locks the enterprise into that vendor's system and eliminates some of the financial benefits and flexibility that cloud computing provides.

- **Data and Application Federation**: Enterprise applications need to combine data from multiple cloud-based sources, and they need to coordinate the activities of applications running in different clouds.

- **SLAs and Benchmarks**: In addition to the basic SLAs required by end users, enterprises who sign contracts based on SLAs will need a standard way of benchmarking performance. There must be an unambiguous way of defining what a cloud provider will deliver, and there must be an unambiguous way of measuring what was actually delivered.

- **Lifecycle Management**: Enterprises must be able to manage the lifecycle of applications and documents. This requirement includes versioning of applications and the retention and destruction of data. Discovery is a major issue for many organizations. There are substantial legal liabilities if certain data is no longer available. In addition to data retention, in some cases an enterprise will want to make sure data is destroyed at some point.

Enterprise to Cloud

This use case involves an enterprise using cloud services for its internal processes. This might be the most common use case in the early stages of cloud computing because it gives the enterprise the most control.

In this scenario, the enterprise uses cloud services to supplement the resources it needs:

- Using cloud storage for backups or storage of seldom-used data
- Using virtual machines in the cloud to bring additional processors online to handle peak loads (and, of course, shutting down those VMs when they're not needed anymore)
- Using applications in the cloud (SaaS) for certain enterprise functions (email, calendaring, CRM, etc.).
- Using cloud databases as part of an application's processing. This could be extremely useful for sharing that database with partners, government agencies, etc.

Requirements

The basic requirements of the Enterprise to Cloud use case are much the same as those for the Enterprise to Cloud to End User use case. An *open client, federated identity, location awareness, metering and monitoring, management and governance, security, a common file format for VMs, common APIs for cloud storage and middleware, data and application federation, SLAs and lifecycle management* all apply.

Other requirements for this use case are:

- *Deployment:* It should be simple to build a VM image and deploy it to the cloud as necessary. When that VM image is built, it should be possible to move that image from one cloud provider to another. Deployment of applications to the cloud should be straightforward as well.
- *Industry-specific standards and protocols:* Many cloud computing solutions between enterprises will use existing standards such as RosettaNet or OAGIS. The applicable standards will vary from one application to the next and from one industry to the next.

Enterprise to Cloud to Enterprise

This use case involves two enterprises using the same cloud. The focus here is hosting resources in the cloud so that applications from the enterprises can interoperate. A supply chain is the most obvious example for this use case.

Requirements

The basic requirements of the Enterprise to Cloud to Enterprise use case are much the same as those for the Enterprise to Cloud use case. *Identity, an open client, federated identity, location awareness, metering and monitoring, management and governance, security, industry-specific standards, common APIs for storage and middleware, data and application federation, SLAs and lifecycle management* all apply. Other requirements for this use case are:

- *Transactions and concurrency:* For applications and data shared by different enterprises, transactions and concurrency are vital. If two enterprises are using the same cloud-hosted application, VM, middleware or storage, it's important that any changes made by either enterprise are done reliably.
- *Interoperability:* Because more than one enterprise is involved, interoperability between the enterprises is essential.

Private Cloud

The Private Cloud use case is different from the others in that the cloud is contained *within* the enterprise. This is useful for larger enterprises. For example, if the payroll department has a surge in workload on the 15th and 30th of each month, they need enough computing power to handle the maximum workload, even though their everyday workload for the rest of the month is much lower. With a private cloud, computing power is spread across the enterprise. The payroll department gets extra cycles when they need it and other departments get extra cycles when they need it. This can deliver significant savings across the enterprise.

Requirements

The basic requirements of the Private Cloud use case are an *open client, metering and monitoring, management and governance, security, deployment, interoperability, a common VM format, and SLAs.*

Note that a private cloud does not require identity, federated identity, location awareness, transactions, industry standards, common APIs for cloud middleware and lifecycle management. In many cases, consumers have to use a private cloud so that location awareness will no longer be an issue. Keeping the cloud inside the enterprise removes many of the requirements for identity management, standards and common APIs.

Changing Cloud Vendors

This use case involves working with a different cloud vendor, either adding an additional vendor or replacing an existing one. It applies to all of the other use cases discussed in this paper. Being able to work with other vendors without major changes is one of the main benefits of openness and standardization.

There are four different scenarios here, each of which has slightly different requirements. In general, changing cloud vendors requires an *open client, location awareness, security, SLAs, a common file format for VMs and common APIs for cloud storage and middleware.* The details of those requirements are discussed in each of the following subsections.

Scenario 1: Changing SaaS vendors

In this scenario a cloud customer changes SaaS vendors. Both SaaS vendors provide the same application (CRM, accounting, word processing, etc.). Documents and data created with one vendor's software should be importable by the second vendor's software. In some cases, the customer might need to use the two vendors interchangeably.

Requirements: Industry-specific standards: Moving documents and data from one vendor's application to another requires both applications to support common formats. The formats involved will depend on the type of application.

In some cases, standard APIs for different application types will also be required: It is important to note that there is nothing cloud-specific to these requirements. The standards for moving a document from Zoho to Google Docs, are the same standards for moving a document from Microsoft Office to OpenOffice.

Scenario 2: Changing middleware vendors

In this scenario a cloud customer changes cloud middleware vendors. Existing data, queries, message queues and applications must be exportable from one vendor and importable by the other.[2]

Requirements:

- *Industry-specific standards:* Moving documents and data from one vendor's middleware to another requires both applications to support common formats. The formats involved will depend on the type of application.
- *Common APIs for Cloud Middleware:* This includes all of the operations supported by today's cloud services, including cloud databases, cloud message queues and other middleware. APIs for connecting to, creating and dropping databases and tables.

Cloud database vendors have enforced certain restrictions to make their products more scalable and to limit the possibility of queries against large data sets taking significant resources to process. For example, some cloud databases don't allow joins across tables, and some don't support a true database schema. Those restrictions are a major challenge to moving between cloud database vendors, especially for applications built on a true relational model.

Other middleware services such as message queues are more similar, so finding common ground among them should be simpler.

Scenario 3: Changing cloud storage vendors

In this scenario a cloud customer changes cloud storage vendors.

Requirements:

- A *Common API for Cloud Storage:* Code that reads or writes data in one cloud storage system should work with a different system with as few changes as possible; those changes should be confined to configuration code. In a JDBC application, as an example, the format of the URL and the driver name are different for different database vendors, but the code to interact with the database is identical.

Scenario 4: Changing VM hosts

In this scenario a cloud customer wants to take virtual machines built on one cloud vendor's system and run it on another cloud vendor's system.

Requirements:

- *A common format for virtual machines:* The VM format should work with any operating system. The assumption here is that the virtual machines themselves are running an operating system such as Windows or Linux. This means that the user of the virtual machine has chosen a platform prior to building a VM for the cloud, so there are no cloud-specific requirements for the software running inside the VM.

Hybrid Cloud

This use case involves multiple clouds working together, including both public and private clouds. A hybrid cloud can be delivered by a federated cloud provider that combines its own resources with those of other providers. A broker can also deliver a hybrid cloud; the difference is that a broker does not have any cloud resources of its own. The provider of the hybrid cloud must manage cloud resources based on the consumer's terms

It is important to note that to the consumer of a hybrid cloud, this use case is no different from the End User to Cloud use case discussed earlier. The user has no knowledge of what the hybrid cloud provider actually does.

Requirements:

- All of the requirements of the previous use cases (except *Transactions and concurrency*) apply here, particularly *Security, Data and Application Federation and Interoperability.*
- *SLAs:* A machine readable, standard format for expressing an SLA. This allows the hybrid cloud provider to select resources according to the consumer's terms without human intervention.

The requirements for a ***community cloud*** are a subset of the requirements for the hybrid cloud. A community cloud has an infrastructure shared among enterprises with a common purpose. The communication between the community and the community cloud is done across an *intranet*. This could be a VPN, but access is not via the public Internet.

The following table summarizes the requirements for all of the use cases:

Requirement	End User to Cloud	Enterprise to Cloud to End User	Enterprise to Cloud	Enterprise to Cloud to Enterprise	Private Cloud	Changing Cloud Vendors	Hybrid Cloud
Identity	✓	✓		✓			✓
Open Client	✓	✓	✓	✓	✓	✓	✓
Federated Identity		✓	✓	✓			✓
Location Awareness		✓	✓	✓		✓	✓
Metering and Monitoring		✓	✓	✓	✓		✓
Management and Governance		✓	✓	✓	✓		✓
Security	✓	✓	✓	✓	✓	✓	✓

Requirement	End User to Cloud	Enterprise to Cloud to End User	Enterprise to Cloud	Enterprise to Cloud to Enterprise	Private Cloud	Changing Cloud Vendors	Hybrid Cloud
Deployment			✓		✓		✓
Transactions and Concurrency				✓			
Interoperability				✓			✓
Industry-Specific Standards			✓	✓			✓
VM Image Format		✓	✓	✓	✓	✓	✓
Cloud Storage API		✓	✓	✓		✓	✓
Cloud Database API		✓	✓	✓		✓	✓
Cloud Middleware API		✓	✓	✓		✓	✓
Data and Application Federation		✓	✓	✓			✓
SLAs	✓	✓	✓	✓	✓	✓	✓
Lifecycle Management		✓	✓	✓			✓

Conclusions and Recommendations

Cloud computing builds on and complements many trends in the industry, including virtualization, SOA and Web 2.0. As a result, standards already exist for many of the requirements outlined in this paper. As we go forward, we will work together as a community to specify the existing standards that meet customer needs, leverage standards work already in progress, and identify what is needed to fill in the gaps not addressed by existing standards.

This paper was created by an open Web community of more than 750 participants. The initial group consisted of supporters from the Open Cloud Manifesto, but it quickly grew to include many other individuals around the world. The community included representatives from large and small companies, government agencies, consultants and vendors.

As the paper was developed, three principles from the manifesto were crucial: 1) users should work together, 2) activities to keep the cloud open should be customer driven and 3) existing standards should be used wherever possible. This paper is validation that those principles work, and they will be central to any follow-on work.

The use cases described here demonstrate the following general requirements:

- *Common VM Formats, Data Formats and APIs:* Virtual machines, data and applications created for one cloud provider should run on another cloud provider without changes.
- *Cloud Management:* Cloud computing is not feasible without service management, governance, metering, monitoring, federated identity, SLAs and benchmarks, data and application federation, deployment, and lifecycle management.
- *Security:* Security in cloud computing is vital, although the requirements for security will vary widely depending on the application and data types.
- *Location awareness:* A way of identifying the location of the physical machine hosting the cloud infrastructure is an absolute requirement for many government regulations.

It must be possible for consumers to implement the use cases outlined here without resorting to closed, proprietary solutions that lead to vendor lock-in. Where existing standards meet requirements, we must ensure those standards are implemented pervasively and consistently. Where existing standards do not meet requirements, we must define and implement the standards needed to meet them. This community-written paper is meant to be the reference for establishing a truly open cloud computing environment.

References.

[1] http://groups.google.com/group/cloud-computing-use-cases

[2] Because of the popularity of cloud storage, cloud middleware (databases, message queues, Map Reduce) and cloud storage are considered separate scenarios, even though both are classified as PaaS.

B. How To Evolve Your Irrelevant Corporate Website

In his personal blog, Forrester Research analyst, Jeremiah Owyang, posted an eye-opening entry, "How To Evolve Your Irrelevant Corporate Website." Jeremiah wrote: [1]

What's a corporate Web site? It's the domain they use after every advertisement where you can learn more about a company, ya know it, anycompany.com. But we're tired of the corporate Website and all its happy marketing speak, stock photos of smart looking dudes or minority women crowded around the computer raving about your product, the positive press release, the happy customer testimonials, the row of executive portraits, the donations your corporate made to disaster relief, the one-sided view never ends.

While some of your traffic may be going up on your Website, it's not indicative of how corporate Websites are being used. Analytics don't tell us *why* people go to your site, and it may not be for the reason you want them to. The corporate Website is an unbelievable collection of hyperbole, artificial branding, and pro-corporate content. As a result, trusted decisions are being made on other locations on the Net.

Why is your corporate Website irrelevant? Marketing has shifted, it's no longer on two domains. Many Web marketers are under the impression that the battles are only fought within Google search results and on the corporate domain. In reality, marketing has spread to many other areas where conversations occur: social networks, rating sites, chat rooms, and even blogs.

Decisions are made before they go to the corporate Web site. Yesterday, at lunch with a college student, she told me that her peers get ideas about product decisions on consumer rating sites, and from their peers. They use instant messaging, Facebook, (and other social networks) and rarely directly type in a domain name to corporate Website. If this holds true, then it's assumed that prospects make decisions on other Websites *before* they come to the corporate Website to get factual information.

Factual information. Legally, corporations need to disclose product details, this is a strong case for the use of the corporate Websites. However in my continued conversation with the Generation Y, she continued to tell me that she used corporate Websites to get core feature stats and pricing, but that's after she made a decision based upon her peer feedback to visit the corporate site.

The future, and how to stay relevant:
▪ *Websites are created with customers:* This is disruptive, but I predict that the most relevant future Websites will have customers building Websites alongside employees. The most effective Websites will contain a balanced point of view of both the product team and customers —even if they have qualms with the product.

▪ *Unfiltered customer testimonials will appear:* You'll no longer be the only one publishing to your Website. Customers, prospects, and other members of the community will have direct access to publish on your Website. Sure, there will be controls to make sure the content is somewhat factual or reviewed, but it will be obvious to many that the only voice won't be the marketing one.

▪ *Content will have both negative and positive views about your products:* This one is hard to swallow, but how do you build the most trust? By being open, authentic, and transparent to the marketplace. We know from research that the highest degree of trust comes from those 'like me', a savvy marketer will allow content to appear from peers, customers, and the market. These will not always be a product rave, in fact it may be downright criticism. The goal? To take that feedback, and demonstrate in public how you will improve your offerings in plain view. Case study: Dell has done this with IdeaStorm.

▪*Your Website will be a Community Resource:* This means that you'll put your customers first. No Really, I mean it. This means providing analysis of not just yourself but of competitors as well. This means that you'll link to competitors. Crazy? I did this in my previous role as a community manager. I created a wiki for customers that linked to competitors, and it made me more relevant.

Outcomes. Customers will make your site the first place to go for information, trust will increase, you may be able to build better products and services with real-time customer feedback, and most importantly, you'll be a community resource that will help you meet your customer needs faster.

Visualize. We'll start to see customers help write the corporate newsletter, feeds pulling in industry blogs, media (audio and video) customers rating and ranking and voting for what features they want improved, product teams working directly with customers in real-time, and customers self-supporting each other.

---

[1] http://www.web-strategist.com/blog/2007/05/29/web-strategy-how-to-evolve-your-irrelevant-corporate-website/

C. Global Collectivist Society Is Coming Online

Kevin Kelly, *Wired* magazine
Summary. Read full article at footnote link. [1]

In his 2008 book, *Here Comes Everybody*, media theorist Clay Shirky suggests a useful hierarchy for sorting through these new social arrangements. Groups start off simply sharing and then progress to cooperation, collaboration, and finally collectivism. At each step, the amount of coordination increases. A survey of the online landscape reveals ample evidence of this phenomenon.

I. Sharing: The online masses have an incredible willingness to share. The number of personal photos posted on Facebook and MySpace is astronomical. Add to this the 6 billion videos served by YouTube each month in the U.S. alone. The list of sharing organizations is almost endless: Yelp for reviews, Loopt for locations, Delicious for bookmarks. Sharing serves as the foundation for higher levels of communal engagement.

II. Cooperation: Not only have amateurs shared more than three billion photos on Flickr, the popularity of Creative Commons licensing means that communally, *your picture is my picture.* I don't have to shoot yet another photo of the Eiffel Tower, since the community can provide a better one than I can take myself. Community aggregators can unleash astonishing power. Sites like Digg and Reddit, which let users vote on the Web links they display most prominently, can steer public conversation as much as newspapers or TV networks. Serious contributors to these sites put in far more energy than they could ever get in return, but they keep contributing in part because of the cultural power these instruments wield.

III. Collaboration: Organized collaboration can produce results beyond the achievements of ad hoc cooperation. Just look at any of hundreds of open source software projects, such as the Apache Web server. In these endeavors, finely tuned communal tools generate high-quality products from the coordinated work of thousands or tens of thousands of members. Instead of money, the peer producers who create the stuff gain credit, status, reputation, enjoyment, satisfaction, and experience. Not only is the product free, it can be copied freely and used as the basis for new products. Alternative schemes for managing intellectual property, including Creative Commons and the GNU licenses, were invented to ensure these "frees."

IV. Collectivism: The aim of a collective is to engineer a system where self-directed peers take responsibility for critical processes. While millions of writers contribute to Wikipedia, a smaller number of editors (around 1,500) are responsible for the majority of the editing. In the past, constructing an organization that exploited hierarchy yet maximized collectivism was nearly impossible. Now digital networking provides the necessary infrastructure. The Net empowers product-focused organizations to function collectively while keeping the hierarchy from fully taking over. Wikipedia is not a bastion of equality, but it is vastly more collectivist than the Encyclopedia Britannica. The elite core we find at the heart of online collectives is actually a sign that stateless socialism can work on a grand scale.

Most people in the West were indoctrinated with the notion that extending the power of individuals necessarily diminishes the power of the state, and vice versa. In practice, though, most polities socialize some resources and individualize others. Most free-market economies have socialized education, and even extremely socialized societies allow some private property.

Rather than viewing technological socialism as one side of a zero-sum trade-off between free-market individualism and centralized authority, it can be seen as a cultural OS that elevates both the individual and the group at once. The largely unarticulated but intuitively understood goal of communitarian technology is this: to maximize both individual autonomy and the power of people working together. Thus, digital socialism can be viewed as a third way that renders irrelevant the old debates.

The notion of a 'third way' is echoed by Yochai Benkler, author of *The Wealth of Networks*,[2] who has probably thought more than anyone else about the politics of networks. "I see the emergence of social production and peer production as an alternative to both state-based and market-based closed, proprietary systems," he says, noting that these activities "can enhance creativity, productivity, and freedom." The new OS is neither the classic communism of centralized planning without private property nor the undiluted chaos of a free market. Instead, it is an emerging design in which decentralized public coordination can solve problems and create things that neither pure communism nor pure capitalism can.

Hybrid systems that blend market and nonmarket mechanisms are not new. For decades, researchers have studied the decentralized, socialized production methods of northern Italian and Basque industrial co-ops, in which employees are owners, selecting management and limiting profit distribution, independent of state control. But only since the arrival of low-cost, instantaneous, ubiquitous collaboration has it been possible to migrate the core of those ideas into diverse new realms, like writing enterprise software or reference books.

Of course, the total census of participants in online collective work is far greater. YouTube claims some 350 million monthly visitors. Nearly 10 million registered users have contributed to Wikipedia, 160,000 of whom are designated active. More than 35 million folks have posted and tagged more than 3 billion photos and videos on Flickr. Yahoo hosts 7.8 million groups focused on every possible subject. Google has 3.9 million.

These numbers still fall short of a nation. They may not even cross the threshold of mainstream (although if YouTube isn't mainstream, what is?). But clearly the population that lives with socialized media is significant. The number of people who make things for free, share things for free, use things for free, belong to collective software farms, work on projects that require communal decisions, or experience the benefits of decentralized socialism has reached millions and counting. Revolutions have grown out of much smaller numbers.

How close to an open source, peer-production society can this movement take us? Every time that question has been asked, the answer has been: closer than we thought. Consider craigslist. Just classified ads, right? But the site amplified the handy community swap board to reach a regional audience, enhanced it with pictures and real-time updates, and suddenly became a national treasure. Operating without state funding or control, connecting citizens directly to citizens, this mostly free marketplace achieves social good at an efficiency that would stagger any government or traditional corporation. Sure, it undermines the business model of newspapers, but at the same time it makes an indisputable case that the sharing model is a viable alternative to both profit-seeking corporations and tax-supported civic institutions.

Who would have believed that poor farmers could secure $100 loans from perfect strangers on the other side of the planet—and pay them back? That is what Kiva does with peer-to-peer lending. Every public health care expert declared confidently that sharing was fine for photos, but no one would share their medical records. But PatientsLikeMe, where patients pool results of treatments to better their own care, prove that collective action can trump both doctors and privacy scares. The increasingly common habit of sharing what you're thinking (Twitter), what you're reading (StumbleUpon), your finances (Wesabe), your everything (the Web) is becoming a foundation of our culture. Doing it while collaboratively building encyclopedias, news agencies, video archives, and software in groups that span continents, with people you don't know and whose class is irrelevant—that makes political socialism seem like the logical next step.

A similar thing happened with free markets over the past century. Every day, someone asked: What can't markets do? We took a long list of problems that seemed to require rational planning or paternal government and instead applied marketplace logic. In most cases, the market solution worked significantly better. Much of the prosperity in recent decades was gained by unleashing market forces on social problems.

Now we're trying the same trick with collaborative social technology, applying digital socialism to a growing list of wishes—and occasionally to problems that the free market couldn't solve—to see if it works. So far, the results have been startling. At nearly every turn, the power of sharing, cooperation, collaboration, openness, free pricing, and transparency has proven to be more practical than we capitalists thought possible. Each time we try it, we find that the power of the new socialism is bigger than we imagined.

We underestimate the power of our tools to reshape our minds. Did we really believe we could collaboratively build and inhabit virtual worlds all day, every day, and not have it affect our perspective? The force of online socialism is growing. Its dynamic is spreading beyond electrons—perhaps into elections.

References.

[1] http://www.wired.com/culture/culturereviews/magazine/17-06/nep_newsocialism

[2] http://www.amazon.com/gp/product/product-descrip-tion/0300125771/ref=dp_proddesc_0?ie=UTF8&n=283155&s=books

D. ROI for Social Networks

In her book, *Share This! How You Will Change the World with Social Networking,* media technologist Deanna Zandt takes on the issue of ROI for Social Networks and Social Media and how to respond to a social outrage:

So now you've learned why it's important for your organization to participate in social media, and you've learned how to get started, but you've got someone in your universe—a higher-up, a funder, an investor—who wants to know what you're getting out of all this chitchat.

ROI (return on investment) typically means what kind of money you're making from all the hoo-hah, but money and fundraising can't be the driving forces within social networks. So let's start by reframing ROI.

Even though many of the tools used in social media are free or very inexpensive, a significant investment of staff time is still involved. That I in ROI means more than just how much it costs to pay for an employee to work in the social network space; it also means how much social capital you're investing in the relationships you're developing.

And the R, as we've said, is not just what kind of funds come out of your social network endeavors. Think of it as the relationships you're building and where you want them to lead. Remember, this is not about broadcasting and marketing; this is about engaging in two-way communication.

It's important to think about how you measure the qualitative aspects of social networks (Do people like you? Do they respond to the work you're doing?), and not just the quantitative ones (How many fans do you have? How much money have you raised?). Qualitative metrics can be tricky, but the first step is making clear decisions about what action you want your community to take.

Here are some examples:

- *Satisfaction.* Don't just look at the number of people talking about your work, but start documenting what they're saying. Is it positive? Neutral? Negative?

- *Authority.* Are they coming to your organization as a resource, looking to you for expertise?
- *Loyalty and trust.* How about repeat performance—is this their first time dealing with you? How often are they returning or interacting?

When working with these measurements, goal setting becomes crucial. It's important to keep your goals very focused, especially when you're starting out. Choose small timeframes—having X positive conversations about your work per week. Also, keep your metrics, to start, within just a couple of services. Decide that you're going to work on your Twitter presence for the next two months and then stick with it, rather than spreading yourself too thin across multiple services.

A few final thoughts to take away as you venture out into the wild world of social media ROI:

- *ROI isn't always about dollars.* It's about social capital, and the goodwill and influence you're able to work with.
- *The more specific you can get, the better.* Make your goals and corresponding metrics direct and clear.
- *Audience, audience, audience.* A reminder: This isn't a broadcast medium, it's a conversational medium. Find people who want to have the conversation with you.
- *Ditch things that don't work.* The low cost of these tools allows you to easily abandon tactics that don't work. Don't think that this means you've failed—it just means that it's time to try the next thing.

E. Web Resources

* Mentioned in the book.

The Enterprise Architecture Network
www.linkedin.com/groups?home=&gid=36781

Cloudbook: Where the Cloud Community Connects
www.cloudbook.net

Cloud Computing, VMware, Virtualization and Enterprise 2.0
Group
www.linkedin.com/groups?home=&gid=45151

Open Source Cloud Computing & Virtualization
www.linkedin.com/groups?home=&gid=45655

Cloud Computing Community
www.linkedin.com/groups?home=&gid=57700

Cloud Computing Group
groups.google.ca/group/cloud-computing

Cloud Computing - SaaS
www.saas-and-cloud-computing.meetup.com

Software as a Service (SaaS) Group
www.linkedin.com/groups?home=&gid=122612

CloudCamp - Unconventional Cloud Computing
www.cloudcamp.org

Cloud Storage
www.linkedin.com/groups?home=&gid=132257

Cloud Harbor Blog
www.cloudharbor.wordpress.com

The Cloudsters
www.linkedin.com/groups?home=&gid=836457

Cloud Computing Interoperability Forum (CCIF)
www.cloudforum.org

Cloud Networking
www.linkedin.com/groups?home=&gid=1099017

* Cloud Security Alliance
www.cloudsecurityalliance.org

Cloud Hosting & Service Providers Forum
www.linkedin.com/groups?home=&gid=1911277

Cloud & SOA Governance and Security Group
www.linkedin.com/groups?home=&gid=2067016

Cloud Computing Marketing, Sales and Business Development
www.linkedin.com/groups?home=&gid=2280125

CloudTweaks
www.cloudtweaks.com

Cloud Vision
www.cloudcomputing-vision.com/

* Distributed Management Task Force
www.dmtf.org

* Hewlett Packard Social Computing Lab
www.hpl.hp.com/research/scl

* IBM- Service Science
www.ibm.com/developerworks/spaces/ssme

* Jericho Forum
www.jerichoforum.org

* Object Management Group (OMG)
www.omg.org

* Open Cloud Consortium
www.opencloudconsortium.org

* Open Cloud Manifesto
www.opencloudmanifesto.org/opencloudmanifesto1.htm

* Open Grid Forum
www.ogf.org

Platform-as-a Service
www.platformasaservice.com

* Storage Networking Industry Association
www.snia.org

F. Jericho Forum Commandments

Security has moved in one form or another to become a mainstream activity just as "across the firewall" activities of one form or another have expanded over recent years. Looking ahead, it is becoming difficult to see the traditional concept of an enterprise firewall—meaning a "boundary fence" around the enterprise with all systems, applications and users protected internally through well managed gateways—that will be able to cope or even be more than just one element in a wider and more systematic approach to securing all the parts of an enterprise environment.

The concept of protecting the parts rather than deploying a boundary perimeter of protection is correctly known as "deparameterization," and was the founding reason for a group of CIOs coming together in January 2004 to explore exactly how this could be made into a commercially viable solution. The group claimed at that time that they were unable to find consultants or vendors who were actively working in this area. They then decided to define the topic and feasible approaches themselves. The group called themselves the "Jericho Forum," in reference to the Biblical city of Jericho and the "walls tumbling down." Right from their very first meeting, the Jericho Forum has acted as an independent forum, but with the support of the Open Group for its administration and other activities.

For the sake of simplicity, many people prefer to use the term "Jericho style security" rather than the complicated term, "deparameterization." Also, the association with Open Group adds value to both sides because the Open Group focuses on work and standards, on "boundaryless information flows," and on the ability to do business across and between enterprises, all of which calls for Jericho style security.

The Jericho Forum board comprises user companies, and as of the March 2009 election, the board will include Boeing, Procter & Gamble, Eli Lilly, Standard Chartered Bank, Dresdner Kleinwort, Rolls Royce, and ICI, with a similar membership of global companies, plus a number of industry vendors and consulting companies.

The latest Jericho Forum paper titled "Collaboration Oriented Architecture," defines the reason why it attracts this high caliber of membership. Enterprises are increasingly making use of various forms of social, Web, and even straight email applications and services. The advent of "Software as a Service" and the possible addition of cloud computing, both of which move whole elements of the enterprise's activities outside its perimeter merely serve to explain why it is now a mainstream topic, with the corresponding rise in the availability of methods, products, and implementations.

The Jericho Forum often uses the analogy of highways going into and out of a city to describe its basic principles. The traditional enterprise firewall approach is likened to having city gates requiring all travelers to be inspected before allowing those with good credentials to pass through, and to building walls along each highway to protect these approved travelers while in transit. At low levels of traffic and for simple well-defined purposes, this method works. However, build up the levels of traffic and the complexity of purposes, it becomes increasingly difficult and expensive to try to handle the flow, and it also becomes a barrier to progress. The Jericho approach is not to protect the highway but to protect the travelers, and their activities by predetermining the risks to each and then allowing the situation to determine the necessary secure outcome.

The Jericho Security Architecture offers a cohesive view of every element based on four distinctive layers, namely, securing the network, securing the host system, securing the application, and securing the data. Within each layer, there is a further definition of the elements, such as the host layer: runtime services and their components, platform services and components, and the operating system. Likewise, the application layer focuses on presentation logic, business logic, and data access logic. The granularity is standardized so that the values applied to each element can be understood by any and all participating parties, that is, everything from an enterprise to a security manager through to any of the myriad of actual business tasks. It is this standardization that provides the flexibility to allow safe participation in business activities.

To make this work, there is a "trust" model based on communities and their logical connections between people, processes, and technology, regardless of device type or location. The trust value is awarded by an enterprise to its various elements, and the relationship between enterprises further determines how much trust to place on each of these values. Currently, all of this relies on the active participation between Jericho Forum members. However, increasingly, when two or more enterprises enter into business trading agreements online, the Jericho Forum approach will be adopted. To aid and simplify adoption, there are seven core process modules, all of which are based on the principle of object orientation and can be used individually, although obviously, it is intended that they should be used in an integrated manner. These comprise authentication, authorization, data classification, encryption, trust repository, end point security, and accounting or audit.

When all of the Jericho elements are taken together and applied systematically, they provide a comprehensive and cohesive secure enterprise environment without the barriers to interacting and doing business with any other entity or enterprise.

The Jericho Forum commandments define both the areas and the principles that must be observed when planning for a de-perimeterized future. While building on "good security," the commandments specifically address those areas of security that are necessary to deliver a de-perimeterized vision. The commandments serve as a benchmark by which concepts, solutions, standards and systems can be assessed and measured.

Fundamentals

1. The scope and level of protection should be specific and appropriate to the asset at risk:

- Business demands that security enables business agility and is cost effective
- Whereas boundary firewalls may continue to provide basic network protection, individual systems and data will need to be capable of protecting themselves.

2. Security mechanisms must be pervasive, simple, scalable and easy to manage:
- Unnecessary complexity is a threat to good security
- Coherent security principles are required which span all tiers of the architecture
- Security mechanisms must scale; from small objects to large objects
- To be both simple and scalable, interoperable security "building blocks" need to be capable of being combined to provide the required security mechanisms

3. Assume context at your peril:
- Security solutions designed for one environment may not be transferable to work in another. Thus it is important to understand the limitations of any security solution
- Problems, limitations and issues can come from a variety of sources, including geographic, legal, technical, acceptability of risk, etc.

Surviving in a Hostile World
4. Devices and applications must communicate using open, secure protocols:
- Security through obscurity is a flawed assumption - secure protocols demand open peer review to provide robust assessment and thus wide acceptance and use
- The security requirements of confidentiality, integrity and availability (reliability) should be assessed and built in to protocols as appropriate, not added-on
- Encrypted encapsulation should only be used when appropriate and does not solve everything

5. All devices must be capable of maintaining their security policy on an untrusted network:
- A "security policy" defines the rules with regard to the protection of the asset
- Rules must be complete with respect to an arbitrary context

- Any implementation must be capable of surviving on the raw Internet, e.g., will not break on any input

The need for trust

6. All people, processes, technology must have declared and transparent levels of trust for any transaction to take place:

- Trust in this context is establishing understanding between contracting parties to conduct a transaction and the obligations this assigns on each party involved
- Trust models must encompass people and organisations, and devices and infrastructure
- Trust level may vary by location, transaction type, user role and transactional risk

7. Mutual trust assurance levels must be determinable:

- Devices and users must be capable of appropriate levels of (mutual) authentication for accessing systems and data
- Authentication and authorisation frameworks must support the trust model

Identity, Management and Federation

8. Authentication, authorization and accountability must interoperate and exchange outside of your area of control:

- People/systems must be able to manage permissions of resources and rights of users they don't control
- There must be capability of trusting an organisation, which can authenticate individuals or groups, thus eliminating the need to create separate identities
- In principle, only one instance of person or system or identity may exist, but privacy necessitates the support for multiple instances, or once instance with multiple facets
- Systems must be able to pass on security credentials and related assertions
- Multiple loci (areas) of control must be supported

Access to data

9. Access to data should be controlled by security attributes of the

data itself:
- Attributes can be held within the data (DRM and Metadata) or could be a separate system
- Access and security could be implemented by encryption
- Some data may have "public, non-confidential" attributes
- Access and access rights have a temporal component

10. Data privacy (and security of any asset of sufficiently high value) requires a segregation of duties and privileges:
- Permissions, keys, privileges and so on must ultimately fall under independent control, or there will always be a weakest link at the top of the chain of trust
- Administrator access must also be subject to these controls

11. By default, data must be appropriately secured when stored, in transit and in use
- Removing the default must be a conscious act
- High security should not be enforced for everything. "Appropriate" implies varying levels with potentially some data not secured at all

Conclusion

De-perimeterization has happened, is happening and is inevitable. Central protection is decreasing in effectiveness It will happen in your corporate lifetime. Therefore you need to plan for it and should have a roadmap of how to get there. The Jericho Forum has a roadmap to assist in the planning.

Refer to www.jerichoforum.org to ensure you have the latest version of the Jericho Forum Commandments.

G. Brief Glossary of NIST Definitions

For a more complete glossary visit:
www.mkpress.com/cloudreading

The NIST definition describes five essential characteristics of Cloud Computing:

1. Rapid Elasticity: Elasticity is defined as the ability to scale resources both up and down as needed. To the consumer, the cloud appears to be infinite, and the consumer can purchase as much or as little computing power as they need.

2. Measured Service: In a measured service, aspects of the cloud service are controlled and monitored by the cloud provider. This is crucial for billing, access control, resource optimization, capacity planning and other tasks.

3. On-Demand Self-Service: The on-demand and self-service aspects of cloud computing mean that a consumer can use cloud services as needed without any human interaction with the cloud provider.

4. Ubiquitous Network Access: Ubiquitous network access means that the cloud provider's capabilities are available over the network and can be accessed through standard mechanisms by both thick and thin clients.[1]

5. Location-Independent Resource Pooling: Resource pooling allows a cloud provider to serve its consumers via a multi-tenant model. Physical and virtual resources are assigned and reassigned according to consumer demand. The location of the physical resources underneath the cloud infrastructure is not known to the consumer, and can change dynamically.[2]

Interoperability: Interoperability is concerned with the ability of systems to communicate. It requires that the communicated information is understood by the receiving system. Interoperability is not concerned with whether the communicating systems do anything sensible as a whole.[3]

Integration: Integration is the process of combining components or systems into an overall system. Integration among cloud-based components and systems can be complicated by issues such as multi-tenancy, federation and government regulations.

Portability: Portability is the ability of moving components or systems between environments. In the world of cloud computing, this includes software and hardware environments (both physical and virtual).

Service Level Agreement (SLA): An SLA is contract between a provider and a consumer that specifies consumer requirements and the provider's commitment to them. Typically an SLA includes items such as uptime, privacy, security and backup procedures.

Federation: Federation is the act of combining data or identities across multiple systems. Federation can be done by a cloud provider or by a cloud broker.

Broker: A broker has no cloud resources of its own, but matches consumers and providers based on the SLA required by the consumer. The consumer has no knowledge that the broker does not control the resources.

Multitenancy: Multitenancy is the property of multiple systems, applications or data from different enterprises hosted on the same physical hardware. Multitenancy is common to most cloud-based systems.

Cloud bursting: Cloud bursting is a technique used by hybrid clouds to provide additional resources to private clouds on an as-needed basis. If the private cloud has the processing power to handle its workloads, the hybrid cloud is not used. When workloads exceed the private cloud's capacity, the hybrid cloud automatically allocates additional resources to the private cloud.

Policy: A policy is a general term for an operating procedure. For example, a security policy might specify that all requests to a particular cloud service must be encrypted.

Governance: Governance refers to the controls and processes that make sure policies are enforced.

Virtual Machine (VM): A file (typically called an image) that, when executed, looks to the user like an actual machine. Infrastructure as a Service is often provided as a VM image that can be started or stopped as needed. Changes made to the VM while it is running can be stored to disk to make them persistent.

---

[1] This does not necessarily mean Internet access. By definition, a private cloud is accessible only behind a firewall. Regardless of the type of network, access to the cloud is typically not limited to a particular type of client.

[2] In many cases privacy laws and other regulations require the cloud provider's resources to be in a particular *location*. The cloud provider and cloud consumer must work together to adhere to those regulations.

[3] The definitions of interoperability, integration and portability are based on the work at http://www.testingstandards.co.uk/interop_et_al.htm.

Bibliography

This bibliography has five categories:
1. **Social Media**
2. **Web 2.0**
3. **Cloud Computing**
4. **Service-Oriented Architecture (SOA)**
5. **Business Process Management (BPM)**

You can find additional books and a hot-linked bibliography at **www.mkpress.com/cloudreading**

Social Media

Bell, Gavin, *Building Social Web Applications: Establishing Community at the Heart of Your Site*, O'Reilly Media, Inc.

Bernal, Joey, *Web 2.0 and Social Networking for the Enterprise: Guidelines and Examples for Implementation and Management Within our Organization*, IBM Press, 2009.

Breslin, John G., Alexandre Passant and Stefen Decker, *The Social Semantic Web*, Springer, 2009.

Brogan, Chris and Julien Smith, *Trust Agents: Using the Web to Build Influence, Improve Reputation, and Earn Trust*, Wiley, 2009.

Brown, Rob, *Public Relations and the Social Web: How to Use Social Media and Web 2.0 in Communications*, Kogan Page, 2009.

Dan Zarrella, *The Social Media Marketing Book*, O'Reilly Media, 2009.

Davies, Julia and Guy Merchant, *Web 2.0 for Schools: Learning and Social Participation*, Peter Lang Publishing, 2009.

Espejo, Roman, *Should Social Networking Web Sites Be Banned?*, Greenhaven Press, 2008.

Evans, Dave, *Social Media Marketing: An Hour a Day*, Sybex, 2008.

Footen, John and Joey Faust, *The Service-Oriented Media Enterprise: SOA, BPM, and Web Services in Professional Media Systems*, Focal Press,

2008.

Gentle, Anne, *Conversation and Community: The Social Web for Documentation*, XML Press, 2009.

Green, Cindy Estis, *The Travel Marketer's Guide to Social Media and Social Networks: Sales and Marketing In A Web 2.0 World*, The HSMAI Foundation, 2007.

Hall, Starr and Chadd Rosenberg, *Get Connected: The Social Networking Toolkit for Business*, Entrepreneur Press, 2009.

Harris, David, *A Key to Successful Intra-Organizational Job Transfers: Social Networks and Webs of Inclusion*, VDM Verlag, 2009.

Hay, Deltina, *A Survival Guide to Social Media and Web 2.0 Optimization: Strategies, Tactics, and Tools for Succeeding in the Social Web*, Dalton Publishing, 2009.

Hoekman, Robert Jr., *Designing the Moment: Web Interface Design Concepts in Action*, New Riders Press, 2008.

Howe, Jeff, *Crowdsourcing: Why the Power of the Crowd Is Driving the Future of Business*, Crown Business, 2008.

Jonghe, An De, *Social Networks Around The World: How is Web 2.0 Changing Your Daily Life?*, BookSurge Publishing, 2008.

Li, Charlene and Josh Bernoff, *Groundswell: Winning in a World Transformed by Social Technologies*, Harvard Business School Press, 2008.

Lincoln, Susan Rice, *Mastering Web 2.0: Transform Your Business Using Key Website and Social Media Tools*, Kogan Page, 2009.

Lytras, Miltiadis D. and Patricia Ordonez de Pablos, *Social Web Evolution: Integrating Semantic Applications and Web 2.0 Technologies*, Information Science Reference, 2009.

Mika, Peter, *Social Networks and the Semantic Web*, Springer, 2007.

Mulholland, Andy and Nick Earle, *Mesh Collaboration*, Evolved Technologist, 2008.

Nguyen, Ngoc Thanh, Ryszard Kowalczyk, and Shyi-Ming,

ChenComputational Collective Intelligence. Semantic Web, Social Networks and Multiagent Systems, Springer, 2009.

Papacharissi, Zizi, *A Networked Self: Identity, Community, and Culture on Social Network Sites,* Routledge, August, 2010.

Porter, Joshua, *Designing for the Social Web,* New Riders Press, 2008.

Safko, Lon and David Brake, *The Social Media Bible: Tactics, Tools, and Strategies for Business Success,* Wiley, 2009.

Shah, Rawn, *Social Networking for Business: Choosing the Right Tools and Resources to Fit Your Needs,* Wharton School Publishing, 2010.

Shih, Clara, *The Facebook Era: Tapping Online Social Networks to Build Better Products, Reach New Audiences, and Sell More Stuff,* Prentice Hall PTR, 2009.

Shirky, Clay, *Here Comes Everybody: The Power of Organizing Without Organizations,* Penguin Press, 2008.

Silver, David, *The Social Network Business Plan: 18 Strategies That Will Create Great Wealth,* Wiley, 2009.

Smith, Gene, *Tagging: People-powered Metadata for the Social Web,* New Riders Press, 2008.

Surowiecki, James, *The Wisdom of Crowds,* Anchor, 2005.

Tuten, Tracy L., *Advertising 2.0: Social Media Marketing in a Web 2.0 World,* Praeger, 2008.

Van Horn, Royal, *TECHNOLOGY: Cookies, Web Profilers, Social Network Cartography, and Proxy Servers.(Internet privacy, security): An article from: Phi Delta Kappan,* Phi Delta Kappa, Inc., 2004.

Vickery, Graham and Sacha Wunsch-Vincent, *Participative Web And User-Created Content: Web 2.0 Wikis and Social Networking,* Organization for Economic Development , 2007.

Watkins, Craig S., *The Young and the Digital: What the Migration to Social Network Sites, Games, and Anytime, Anywhere Media Means for Our Future,* Beacon Press, 2009.

Weber, Larry, *Marketing to the Social Web: How Digital Customer Com-*

munities Build Your Business, Wiley, 2009.

Weber, Steve, *Plug Your Business! Marketing on MySpace, YouTube, blogs and podcasts and other Web 2.0 social networks,* Weber Books, 2007.

Weinberg, Tamar, *The New Community Rules: Marketing on the Social Web,* O'Reilly Media, Inc., 2009.

Web 2.0

Bell, Ann, *Exploring Web 2.0: Second Generation Interactive Tools - Blogs, Podcasts, Wikis, Networking, Virtual Words, And More,* CreateSpace, 2009.

Berger, Pam and Sally Trexler, *Choosing Web 2.0 Tools for Learning and Teaching in a Digital World,* Libraries Unlimited, 2010. (to be released in April, 2010)

Burrows, Terry, *Blogs, Wikis, MySpace, and More: Everything You Want to Know About Using Web 2.0 but Are Afraid to Ask,* Chicago Review Press, 2008.

Carter, Sandy, *The New Language of Business: SOA & Web 2.0,* IBM Press, 2007.

Casarez, Vince, Billy Cripe, Jean Sini and Philipp Weckerle, *Reshaping Your Business with Web 2.0: Using New Social Technologies to Lead Business Transformation,* McGraw-Hill Osborne Media, 2008.

Coleman, David and Stewart Levine, *Collaboration 2.0: Technology and Best Practices for Successful Collaboration in a Web 2.0 World,* Happy About, 2008.

Evans, Alan and Diane M. Coyle, *Introduction to Web 2.0,* Prentice Hall, 2009.

Funk, Tom, *Web 2.0 and Beyond: Understanding the New Online Business Models, Trends, and Technologies,* Praeger , 2008.

Goto, Kelly and Cotler Emily, *Web ReDesign 2.0: Workflow that Works,* Peachpit Press, 2004.

Governor, James, Dion Hinchcliffe and Duane Nickull, *Web 2.0*

Architectures: What entrepreneurs and information architects need to know, O'Reilly, 2009.

Jesse, Feiler, *How to Do Everything with Web 2.0 Mashups,* McGraw-Hill Osborne Media, 2007.

Jones, Bradley L.,*Web 2.0 Heroes: Interviews with 20 Web 2.0 Influencers,* Wiley, 2008.

Hay, Deltina, *A Survival Guide to Social Media and Web 2.0 Optimization: Strategies, Tactics, and Tools for Succeeding in the Social Web,* Dalton Publishing, 2009.

Kaushik, Avinash, *Web Analytics 2.0: The Art of Online Accountability and Science of Customer Centricity,* Sybex, 2009.

Lanclos, Patsy and David Hoerger, *Weaving Web 2.0 Tools into the Classroom,* Visions Technology in Education, 2008.

McAfee, Andrew, *Enterprise 2.0: New Collaborative Tools for Your Organization's Toughest Challenges,* Harvard Business School Press, 2009.

O'Reilly, *Web 2.0 Principles and Best Practices,* O'Reilly Media, 2006.

Raymond, Yee, *Pro Web 2.0 Mashups: Remixing Data and Web Services,* Apress, 2008.

Richardson, Will, *Blogs, Wikis, Podcasts, and Other Powerful Web Tools for Classrooms,* Corwin Press, 2008.

Rigby, Ben, *Mobilizing Generation 2.0: A Practical Guide to Using Web2.0 Technologies to Recruit, Organize and Engage Youth,* Jossey-Bass, 2008.

Scott, Bill and Theresa Neil, *Designing Web Interfaces: Principles and Patterns for Rich Interactions,* O'Reilly Media, 2009.

Segaran, Toby, *Programming Collective Intelligence: Building Smart Web 2.0 Applications,* O'Reilly Media, Inc., 2007.

Sankar, Krishna and Susan A. Bouchard, *Enterprise Web 2.0 Fundamentals,* Cisco, 2009.

Shuen, Amy, *Web 2.0: A Strategy Guide: Business thinking and strategies behind successful Web 2.0 implementations,* O'Reilly Media, Inc., 2009.

Solomon, Gwen and Lynne Schrum, *Web 2.0: New Tools, New Schools,* International Society for Technology in Education, 2007.

Tuten, Tracy L., *Advertising 2.0: Social Media Marketing in a Web 2.0 World,* Praeger, 2008.

Vlist, Eric van der, Danny Ayers, Erik Bruchez, Joe Fawcett and Alessandro Vernet, *Professional Web 2.0 Programming,* Wrox, 2006.

Vossen, Gottfried and Stephan Hagemann, *Unleashing Web 2.0: From Concepts to Creativity,* Morgan Kaufmann, 2007.

Zabir, Omar AL, *Building a Web 2.0 Portal with ASP.Net 3.5: None,* O'Reilly Media, 2008.

Zervaas, Quentin, *Practical Web 2.0 Applications with PHP,* Apress, 2007.

Cloud Computing

Ahson, Syed A., *Cloud Computing and Software Services: Theory and Techniques,* CRC, 2009.

Beard, Haley, *Cloud Computing Best Practices for Managing and Measuring Processes for On-demand Computing, Applications and Data centers in the Cloud with SLAs,* Emereo Pty Ltd, 2008.

Benioff, Marc and Carlye Adler, *Behind the Cloud: The Untold Story of How Salesforce.com Went from Idea to Billion-Dollar Company and Revolutionized an Industry,* Jossey-Bass, 2009.

Beswick, James, *Getting Productive With Google Apps: Increase productivity while cutting costs,* 415 Systems, Inc. 2009.

Buckley, Peter, *The Rough Guide to Cloud Computing,* Rough Guides, 2010.

Chou, Timothy, *Cloud: Seven Clear Business Models,* LuLu Press, 2009.

Fida, Adnan, *Workflow Scheduling for Service Oriented Cloud Computing: cloud, grid, scheduling, services, simulation, workflows,* VDM Verlag Dr. Müller, 2009.

Fingar, Peter, *Dot Cloud: The 21st Century Business Platform Built on Cloud Computing,* Meghan-Kiffer Press, 2009.

Franklin, Curtis Jr. and Brian Chee, *Cloud Computing: Technologies and Strategies of the Ubiquitous Data Center,* CRC, 2010.

Granneman, Scott, *Google Apps Deciphered: Compute in the Cloud to Streamline Your Desktop,* Prentice Hall PTR, 2008.

Greenfield, Adam, *Everyware: The Dawning Age of Ubiquitous Computing,* New Riders Publishing, 2006.

Greer, Melvin B. Jr. *Software as a Service Inflection Point: Using Cloud Computing to Achieve Business Agility,* iUniverse, 2009.

Hoff, Christofer, Rich Mogull, and Craig Balding, *Hacking Exposed: Virtualization & Cloud Computing: Secrets & Solutions,* McGraw-Hill Osborne Media, October 2010.

Hurwitz, Judith, Robin Bloor, Marcia Kaufman and Fern Halper, *Cloud Computing For Dummies,* For Dummies, 2009.

Jennings, Roger, *Cloud Computing with the Windows Azure Platform,* Wrox, 2009.

Katz, Richard N. and Diana G. Oblinger, *The Tower and the Cloud: Higher Education in the Age of Cloud Computing,* EDUCAUSE , 2008.

Krutz, Ronald L. and Russell Dean Vines, *Cloud Security: A Comprehensive Guide to Secure Cloud Computing,* Wiley, August, 2010.

Linthicum, David S., *Cloud Computing and SOA Convergence in Your Enterprise: A Step-by-Step Guide,* Addison-Wesley Professional, 2009.

Marks, Eric A. and Bob Lozano, *Executive's Guide to Cloud Computing,* Wiley, 2010.

Mather, Tim, Subra Kumaraswamy and Shahed Latif, *Cloud Security and Privacy: An Enterprise Perspective on Risks and Compliance (Theory in Practice),* O'Reilly Media, 2009.

McDonald, Kevin T., *Above the Clouds: Managing Risk in the World of Cloud Computing,* IT Governance Publishing, 2010.

Menken, Ivanka, *Cloud Computing - The Complete Cornerstone Guide to*

Cloud Computing Best Practices Concepts, Terms, and Techniques for Successfully Planning, Implementing and Managing Enterprise IT Cloud Computing Technology, Emereo Pty Ltd, 2008.

Miller, Michael, *Cloud Computing: Web-Based Applications That Change the Way You Work and Collaborate Online,* Que, 2008.

Murty, James, *Programming Amazon Web Services: S3, EC2, SQS, FPS, and SimpleDB,* O'Reilly Media, Inc., 2008.

Ouellette, Jason, *Development with the Force.com Platform: Building Business Applications in the Cloud,* Addison-Wesley Professional, 2009.

Reese, George, *Cloud Application Architectures: Building Applications and Infrastructure in the Cloud,* O'Reilly Media, Inc., 2009.

Rhoton, John, *Cloud Computing Explained: Implementation Handbook for Enterprises,* Recursive Press, 2009.

Rittinghouse, John and James Ransome, *Cloud Computing: Implementation, Management, and Security,* CRC, 2009.

Sapir, Jonathan, *Power in the Cloud: Using Cloud Computing to Build Information Systems at the Edge of Chaos,* Meghan-Kiffer Press, 2009.

Sarna, David E. Y., *Implementing and Developing Cloud Computing Applications,* Auerbach Pub, October, 2010.

Velte,Toby, Anthony Velte and Robert Elsenpeter, *Cloud Computing, A Practical Approach,* McGraw-Hill Osborne Media, 2009.

White, Tom, *Hadoop: The Definitive Guide,* O'Reilly Media, Inc., 2009.

Wohl, Amy, *Succeeding at SaaS: Computing in the Cloud,* Wohl Associates, 2008.

Service-Oriented Architecture (SOA)

Amberpoint Inc., et al., *An Implementor's Guide to Service Oriented Architecture - Getting It Right ,* Westminster Promotions, 2008.

Bell, Michael, *Service-Oriented Modeling (SOA): Service Analysis, Design, and Architecture,* Wiley, 2008.

Bertino, Elisa, Lorenzo Martino, Federica Paci and Anna Squiccia-rini, *Security for Web Services and Service-Oriented Architectures,* Springer, 2009.

Bieberstein, Norbert, Sanjay Bose, Marc Fiammante, Keith Jones and Rawn Shah, *Service-Oriented Architecture (SOA) Compass: Business Value, Planning, and Enterprise Roadmap,* IBM Press, 2005.

Biske, Todd, *SOA Governance,* Packt Publishing, 2008.

Carter, Sandy, *The New Language of Business: SOA and Web 2.0,* IBM Press, 2007.

Christudas, Binildas A., Malhar Barai and Vincenzo Caselli, *Service Oriented Architecture with Java: Using SOA and web services to build power-ful Java applications,* Packt Publishing, 2008.

Erl, Thomas, et al, *Web Service Contract Design and Versioning for SOA,* Prentice Hall PTR, 2008.

Erl, Thomas, *Service-Oriented Architecture (SOA): Concepts, Technology, and Design,* Prentice Hall PTR, 2005.

Erl, Thomas, *Service-Oriented Architecture: A Field Guide to Integrating XML and Web Services,* Prentice Hall PTR , 2004.

Erl, Thomas, *SOA Design Patterns,* Prentice Hall PTR; 1 edition, 2009.

Erl, Thomas, *SOA Principles of Service Design,* Prentice Hall PTR; 1 edition, 2007.

Gabhart, Kyle and Bibhas Bhattacharya, *Service Oriented Architecture Field Guide for Executives,* Wiley, 2008.

Graham, Ian, Managing *Service Oriented Architecture Projects With Agile Processes,* John Wiley & Sons, May 2010.

Hasan, Jeffrey and Mauricio Duran, *Expert Service-Oriented Architec-ture in C#,* Apress; 2 edition, 2006.

Hewitt, Eben, *Java Soa Cookbook,* O'Reilly Media, 2009.

Hurwitz, Judith, Robin Bloor, Marcia Kaufman and Fern Halper, *Service Oriented Architecture (SOA) For Dummies, 2nd Edition,* For

Dummies; 2nd edition, 2009.

Josuttis, Nicolai M., *SOA in Practice: The Art of Distributed System Design*, O'Reilly Media, Inc., 2007.

Juneja, Girish, Blake Dournaee, Joe Natoli and Steve Birkel, *Service Oriented Architecture Demystified: A pragmatic approach to SOA for the IT executive*, Intel Press, 2007.

Krafzig, Dirk, Karl Banke and Dirk Slama, *Enterprise SOA: Service-Oriented Architecture Best Practices*, Prentice Hall PTR , 2004.

Lawler, James P. and H. Howell-Barber, *Service-Oriented Architecture: SOA Strategy, Methodology, and Technology*, Auerbach Publications, 2007.

Marks, Eric A. and Michael Bell, *Service-Oriented Architecture (SOA): A Planning and Implementation Guide for Business and Technology*, Wiley, 2006.

Marks, Eric A., *Service-Oriented Architecture (SOA) Governance for the Services Driven Enterprise*, Wiley, 2008.

McGovern, James, Oliver Sims, Ashish Jain and Mark Little, *Enterprise Service Oriented Architectures: Concepts, Challenges, Recommendations*, Springer, 2006.

Melvin, Greer B. Jr., *The Web Services and Service Oriented Architecture Revolution: Using Web Services to Deliver Business Value*, iUniverse, Inc., 2006.

Mulholland, Andy, C. S. Thomas, and P. Kurchina, *Mashup Corporations: The End of Business as Usual*, Evolved Technologist, 2008.

Rosen, Michael, Boris Lublinsky, Kevin T. Smith and Marc J. Balcer, *Applied SOA: Service-Oriented Architecture and Design Strategies*, Wiley, 2008.

Sims, Oliver, Ashish Jain and Mark Little, *Enterprise Service Oriented Architectures: Concepts, Challenges, Recommendations*, Springer Netherlands, 2009.

Suzuki, Junichi, *Developing Effective Service Oriented Architectures: Concepts and Applications in Service Level Agreements, Quality of Service and*

Reliability, Information Science Publishing, July 2010.

Sweeney, Rick, *Achieving Service-Oriented Architecture: Applying an Enterprise Architecture Approach*, Wiley, June 2010.

Thuraisingham, Bhavani, *Security for Service Oriented Architectures*, Auerbach Publications, March, 2010.

Business Process Management

Antonucci, Yvonne Lederer, et al, *Business Process Management Common Body Of Knowledge*, CreateSpace, 2009.

Burlton, Roger, *Business Process Management: Profiting From Process*, Sams, 2001.

Business Process Management Group, *In Search Of BPM Excellence: Straight From The Thought Leaders*, Meghan-Kiffer Press, 2008.

Chang, James, F., *Business Process Management Systems: Strategy and Implementation*, Auerbach Publications, 2005.

Debevoise, Tom, *Business Process Management with a Business Rules Approach: Implementing The Service Oriented Architecture*, BookSurge Publishing, 2007.

Demelio, Robert, *Basics of Process Mapping*, Productivity Press, 1996.

Dickstein, Dennis I. and Robert H. Flast, *No Excuses: A Business Process Approach to Managing Operational Risk*, Wiley, 2008.

Fiammante, Marc, *Dynamic SOA and BPM: Best Practices for Business Process Management and SOA Agility*, IBM Press, 2009.

Fingar, Peter, *Extreme Competition: Innovation And the Great 21st Century Business Reformation*, Meghan-Kiffer Press, 2008.

Fingar, Peter, *The Real-Time Enterprise : Competing on Time*, Meghan-Kiffer Press, 2004.

Garimella, Kiran, *The Power of Process: Unleashing the Source of Competitive Advantage*, Meghan-Kiffer Press, 2006.

Grosskopf, et al, *The Process: Business Process Modeling using BPMN*, Meghan-Kiffer Press, 2009.

Harmon, Paul, *Business Process Change, Second Edition: A Guide for Business Managers and BPM and Six Sigma Professionals,* Morgan Kaufmann, 2007.

Harrison-Broninski, Keith, *Human Interactions: The Heart And Soul Of Business Process Management,* Meghan-Kiffer Press, 2005.

Jeston, John, *Beyond Business Process Improvement, On To Business Transformation: A Manager's Guide,* Meghan-Kiffer Press, 2009.

Jeston, John and Johan Nelis, *Business Process Management, Second Edition: Practical Guidelines to Successful Implementations,* Butterworth-Heinemann, 2008.

Jeston, John and Johan Nelis, *Management by Process: A practical roadmap to sustainable Business Process Management,* Butterworth-Heinemann, 2008.

Khan, Rashid N., *Business Process Management: A Practical Guide,* Meghan-Kiffer Press, 2004.

Madison, Dan, *Process Mapping, Process Improvement and Process Management,* Paton Press, 2005.

Ould, Martin A., *Business Process Management: A Rigorous Approach,* Meghan-Kiffer Press, 2005.

Schurter, Terry, *The Insiders' Guide to BPM: 7 Steps to Process Mastery,* Meghan-Kiffer Press, 2010.

Schurter, Terry, *Customer Expectation Management: Success Without Exception,* Meghan-Kiffer Press, 2006.

Sharp, Alec and Patrick McDermott, *Workflow Modeling,* Artech House Publishers, 2008.

Smith, Howard and Peter Fingar, *Business Process Management: The Third Wave,* Meghan-Kiffer Press, 2006.

Smith, Howard and Peter Fingar, *IT Doesn't Matter-Business Processes Do,* Meghan-Kiffer Press, 2003.

Spanyi, Andrew, *Business Process Management (BPM) is a Team Sport: Play it to Win!,* Meghan-Kiffer Press, 2003.

Spanyi, Andrew, *More for Less: The Power of Process Management,* Meghan-Kiffer Press, 2008.

Thompson, Ken, *The Networked Enterprise: Competing for the Future Through Virtual Enterprise Networks,* Meghan-Kiffer Press, 2008.

Thompson, Ken, *Bioteams: High Performance Teams Based on Nature's Most Successful Designs,* Meghan-Kiffer Press, 2008.

Weske, Mathias, *Business Process Management: Concepts, Languages, Architectures,* Springer Berlin Heidelberg, 2009.

Index

3

30-Day Blitz 197
37 signals 82

A

abstraction 42
adaptive 126
Adobe Systems 147
advertising 78
Agile Development 141
agile enterprise 178
Akerlof, George 65
Alan Kay, ... 54
Amazon 54
Animal Spirits 65
Animoto 54, 185
Applegate, Lynda 53
appliance 40
appliance-based software
    delivery (AbSD) 40
application service provider
    (ASP) 46
applications 89, 92
assessment 186
asymmetric information 65
auditability 138
automobile 101
autonomic 35

B

Bakas, Adjiedj 52
bandwidth 51
bar-code reader 99
Bechtel 120

Benkler, Yochai 58
Berners-Lee, Tim 41
*Beyond the Crisis: The Future of
    Capitalism* 52
Boston Consulting Group . 102
BPMN 34
Business Activity Monitoring
    (BAM) 34, 140
business innovation on
    demand 52
business leadership activities
    149
Business Operations Platform
    (BOP) 34, 46, 136, 147
business process 158
Business Process Execution
    Language (BPEL) 111
Business Process Management
    (as a Service (BPMaaS) 32
Business Process Management
    (BPM) 52, 131
Business Process Management
    as a Service (BPMaaS) 20,
    46, 143
Business Process Management
    System (BPMS) 34, 133
*Business Process Management, A
    Rigorous Approach* 183
*Business Process Management: The
    Third Wave* 33, 157
Business Process Outsourcing
    (BPO) 34
Business Process
    Reengineering (BPR) 89
business processes 86, 115, 133

Business Technology (BT).. 19, 87, 93, 107, 121, 131
Business-IT Gap 133
Bussemaker, Frits 82

C

Cearley, David 193
Chambers, John 5
change 172, 195
Cheney, Paul 68
Chief Process Officer 52
choreography 137, 147, 161
CIO 91, 146, 166
CIO Magazine 168
Cisco 5
cloud brokerage 36, 105
cloud computing 17, 23, 89
cloud computing (def.) ...26, 41
cloud computing Framework
.... 27
Cloud Security and Privacy 191
Cloud Service Provider (CSP)
.... 24, 34
Cloud-Oriented Business
Architecture (COBA) 182
cloudsourced 71
collaboration .. 52, 72, 115, 128
Collaborative Management.. 87
collective intelligence 52
collectivism 67
command and control IT
architecture 35
communications revolutions
.... 81, 170, 202
community cloud 34
community clouds 38
competitive differentiator .. 122
compliance ... 86, 112, 124, 138
Composite Application

Framework (CAF) 140
computer utility 45
computer utility redux 48
consumer IT 41
Consumer IT 16, 85, 93
consumers 105
continuous process
improvement 185, 199
conversation 68
cooperations 83
co-production 160
Cordys 46
corporate social networking
.... 103
cost cutting 88
creative breakthroughs 71
critical success factors 199
Cronkite, Walter 63
crowdsearching 74
crowdsourcing 74

D

Daniels, Russ 51
dark fiber 48
data center consolidation ... 109
data processing 89
delivery model 24, 41
delivery models 28
Dell 67, 122, 157, 194
Dell IdeaStorm 69
demand pull 43, 78
democratization of the press 66
deployment models 38
Desktop as a Service (DaaS) 24
DimDim.com 185
Documents ToGo 97
due diligence 165
Dynabook 54

E

early adopters 112
eBay 79
edge of the enterprise 125
EDS 157
elastic scalability 51
email 75, 86
emergent systems 123
end-to-end situational business
    processes 144
Enterprise Application
    Integration (EAI) .. 120, 134
Enterprise Architecture 116,
    180
enterprise cloud computing. 18
Enterprise IT 85, 93
Enterprise Service Bus (ESB)
    111
entry condition 153
Everything as a Service. 28
exceptions 154
exponential growth curve 48
extended enterprise 111
extended usage patterns 174

F

Facebook 63, 68
Flickr 67
Forrester 69, 107, 120
Fourth Estate 63
front office 87, 121

G

Gage, John 48
Gartner 47, 51, 74, 123, 193
GE Global Research 158
Gelernter, David 4, 80, 101
General Electric 3, 24
George Stalk 4, 49

G

Gerstner, Lou 157
globalization 80
GM 79
Google 55, 64, 100, 176
governance ... 67, 105, 138, 174
Granovetter, Mark 72

H

happy path 154
Harrison-Broninski, Keith. 161
Heffner, Randy 120
Hewlett-Packard 50
Hooper, Grace 4, 67
Human Interactions 161
human-to-human interactions
    161
hybrid cloud 39

I

IBM 156, 158, 194
IDC 50, 187
Ideastorm.com 194
identity 99
Immelt, Jeffrey 3
in the know 61
inbound marketing 78
incremental delivery 199
information spaces 73
Information Technology (IT)
    89
infrastructure 132
Infrastructure as a Service
    (IaaS) 29
innovation 73
integration 106
Intel 76
intellectual property 58, 87
InterCloud 50
Internation 78

Internet 58
Intuit 70
iPhone 97, 105
IT architecture 117
ITIL (Information
Technology Infrastructure
Library) 181

J

Jericho Forum 190
JetBlue 67
Johnson, Maryfran 168

K

Kelly, Kevin 67
Khan, Rashid 148
knowing 61
Knowing Knowledge, ... 61
knowledge 61
knowledge transfer 178
knowledge workers 154
Koulopoulos, Thomas 5
Kundra, Vivek 3

L

lean and mean 103
learn and leverage 114
legacy systems 110, 126, 194
Location independent
resource pooling 27
location-aware 101
loosely coupled 121

M

Management Controls as a
Service (MCaaS) 34
market capability model 115
Master Data Management
(MDM) 140

Matrix Management 86, 87
McKinsey 50
measured service 28
mesh 86
messaging 99
micro blogging 74
middle-out enterprise
architecture 122
Mind-Inside-the-Head
[MITH] model 71
minicomputer 45
*Mirror Worlds: or the Day
Software Puts the Universe in a
Shoebox.* 80
Mobile Social Web 78
mobile society 101
Mobile World Congress 2010
.... 100
mobility 96
monolithic applications 43
Morris, Robert 158
multichannel strategy 110
multitenancy 45

N

narrowcast 70
National Institute of Standards
and Technology (NIST) . 17,
26
news 78
newspapers 79
Ning.com 66
non-core activities 115

O

Object Management Group
(OMG) 128
Ogle, Richard 73
Ogle's laws for Social

Networks 73
On-demand self-service 27
open source software 111
open standards 110
operational efficiency 89
OPEX 90
orchestration 147
organic processes 161
organization 132
Organization for the
    Advancement of Structured
    Information Standards
    (OASIS) 128
organizational hierarchies .. 102
Ould, Martyn 183
outbound marketing 78
outside-in 113, 118
Owyang, Jeremiah 66, 69

P

P2P banking 103
Page-Jones, Meiler 178
participatory society 66
pay-as-you-go 43
pay-per-drink cost savings . 109
Perot Systems 157
personal use 105
personalization 97
Platform as a Service (PaaS) 30
plug and play 114
Plummer, Daryl 51
policy management 105
Power in the Cloud: Building
    Information Systems at the Edge
    of Chaos 142
presence 100
privacy 186
process models 135
Process on Demand 151

Process-Oriented Architecture
    (POA) 181
product lifecycle management
    (PLM) 25
proof-of-concept project ... 196
prosumer 69, 148
provisioning 124
public cloud 39
puncutuated equilibrium 149

Q

QuickBooks 70

R

rapid elasticity 27
rapid Innovation 137
reputations 66
RFID tags 80
Rifkin, Jeremy 80, 170
Robertson, Bruce 123
ROI 68, 136
RSS feed 75

S

safety stock 159
Salesforec.com 46
Sapir, Jonathan 142
Sarbanes-Oxley 46
Schmidt, Eric 100
Schwartz, Johnathan 69
scientific management 103
Second Life 73, 194
security 186
Seely Brown, John 118, 162
sense and respond 114
sensor 62
sentiment 68
service process management
    161

service science......................158
service value chain 159
Service-Oriented Architecture
    (SOA)........ 48, 111, 117, 181
service-oriented computing. 85
Service-Oriented Enterprise
    (SOE)...... 19, 109, 112, 114,
    125
Service-Oriented
    Infrastructure........... 85, 123
services..92, 111, 124, 137, 173
Services Integrators..............106
services processes.................161
services sector.......................156
Services-as-a-Service...........156
Shiller, Robert.........................65
Siemens, George....................61
silos...113
situational applications 141
Situational Business Processes
    (SBPs)...............143, 174,183
smart business services.........90
Smart Phone.................. 96, 100
*Smart World: Breakthrough
    Creativity and the New Science
    of Ideas*.................................73
Smith, Howard 157
SOA Governance Framework
   181
social constructionism....65, 78
Social Media...........................66
Social Networking.... 66, 75, 78
Social Networks................58, 86
Social Software 66
Social Web................ 65, 66, 71
Software as a Service (SaaS) 30,
    46
Software-Platform-
    Infrastructure (SPI) stack 34

Soley, Richard 193
spaghetti code 110
spreadsheets 141
sServices.................................105
Stalk, George..........................102
Stiglitz, Joseph 65
Strategic Business Modeling
    (SBM)..............................150
strategy...................................132
strong ties 72
sub-processes 152
Sun Microsystems 69, 190
supercomputing resources... 51
supply push 43, 78

T

Telxon.......................................98
the bullwhip effect..............159
*The Engineering of Customer
    Services*.................................158
*The Greatest Innovation Since the
    Assembly Line* 197
the Human Network 102
The Human Network...........57
the network is the computer 48
The Networked Enterprise 54
The Open Group 128, 180
The Open Group Architectual
    Framework (TOGAF)...180
The Uptime Institute............50
The World is Flat?....................80
Third Industrial Age 82
Thomas Manes, Anne 118
Thompson, Ken 54
timesharing............................45
time-to-value.........................136
traditional IT..........................89
trust 36, 63, 78, 82
Twitter......... 61, 67, 68, 74, 103

U

Ubiquitous network access .. 27
unified communications 99
unified messaging 100
unintended context 174
UPS 145
use cases 42, 44
users 105

V

value 88, 97
value chains 144
value delivery system ... 53, 149
van der Reep, Frans 102
virality 68
virtual enterprise networks . 54, 87
virtual machine 29
virtual private cloud 38
virtualization 51, 89, 124
Vivek Kundra 3

W

Wal-Mart 69, 98

Watson Research Lab 158

weak ties 72
Web 1.0 75
Web 2.0 .. 41, 43, 49, 62, 75, 85, 89, 121, 148
Web Services 111
Whole Foods 68
Wikipedia 67
wireless device 97
wisdom of crowds 52
Wladawsky-Berger, Irving . 156
workflow 72, 134, 161

X

Xerox 162

Y

Y2K 55, 132
Yammer 103
YOU are the Web 82

Z

Zandt, Deanna 69

About the Authors

ANDY MULHOLLAND joined Capgemini in 1996, bringing with him thirteen years of experience from previous senior IT roles across in all major industry sectors. In his current role as Global Chief Technology Officer Andy advises the Capgemini Group management board on all aspects of technology-driven market changes, as well as serving on the technology advisory boards of several organizations and enterprises, and being a member of the Policy Board for the British Computer Society. In 2006, Andy drew on his wealth of knowledge of Web 2.0 and Service Oriented Architecture technologies and coauthored the globally recognized book *Mashup Corporations* writing with his Chris Thomas of Intel. This was followed in May 2008 by *Mesh Collaboration* with Nick Earl of Cisco as his co-author. In 2009 Andy was voted one of the top 25 most influential CTOs in the world by *InfoWorld*, and his CTO blog was voted best Blog for Business Managers and CIOs for the second year running by *Computing Weekly* in 2009. His first white paper on Cloud computing, coauthored with Russ Daniels, CTO of HP, was published in December 2008.

JON PYKE has over 30 years experience in the field of software engineering and product development. During his career he has served with a number of software and hardware companies as well as user organizations. Jon is one of the most influential figures in the Business Process Management (BPM) sector. As CTO of Staffware plc (now Tibco) for over 12 years, he can truly claim to be one of the founders of BPM as a means to implement a process improvement culture in business. He was personally responsible for defining many of the key software metaphors that enable BPM to work, and as Chair of the Workflow Management Coalition (WfMC), he has also overseen the development of related standards. As one of BPM's great thinkers, he has written and published a number of articles on the subject of Office Automation, BPM and Workflow Technology. Jon coauthored a book covering both technical and business aspects of BPM, *Mastering Your Organi-*

zation's Processes. Jon demonstrates an exceptional blend of business and people management skills and he is a master technician with a highly developed sense of where technologies fit and how they should be utilized. Jon is a globally recognized industry figure, an exceptional public speaker and a seasoned company executive.

PETER FINGAR, Executive Partner in the business strategy firm, Greystone Group, is one of the industry's noted experts on business process management, and a practitioner with over thirty years of hands-on experience at the intersection of business and technology. Equally comfortable in the boardroom, the computer room or the classroom, Peter has taught graduate computing studies in the U.S. and abroad. He has held management, technical and advisory positions with GTE Data Services, American Software and Computer Services, Saudi Aramco, EC Cubed, the Technical Resource Connection division of Perot Systems and IBM Global Services. He developed technology transition plans for clients served by these companies, including GE, American Express, MasterCard and American Airlines-Sabre. In addition to numerous articles and professional papers, he is an author of nine landmark books, including *Dot.Cloud: The 21st Century Business Platform* and *Business Process Management: The Third Wave.* Peter has delivered keynote talks and papers to professional conferences in America, Austria, Australia, Canada, China, The Netherlands, South Africa, Japan, United Arab Emirates, Saudi Arabia, Egypt, Bahrain, Germany, Britain, Italy and France.